The Best of Epicure's *Gujarati* Cuisine

ASHA KHATAU

Popular Prakashan
www.popularprakashan.com

Published by
POPULAR PRAKASHAN PVT. LTD.
301, Mahalaxmi Chambers
22, Bhulabhai Desai Road
Mumbai – 400 026

First Published 2012

(4424)
ISBN: 978-81-7991-676-6

Design: Mahendra Ghanekar, Anjali Sawant
Typesetting: Vineet Gada
Food Styling: Asha Khatau

Printed in India
at Thomson Press (India) Ltd.
New Delhi

Published by
Harsha Bhatkal for
POPULAR PRAKASHAN PVT. LTD.
301, Mahalaxmi Chambers
22, Bhulabhai Desai Road
Mumbai – 400 026

Dedication

I dedicate this book to Vinodji and Abhaji Singhania,
who have always enjoyed our Gujarati food.

Acknowledgements

I want to thank the One above who gave me the capacity to create yet another book.

My sincere thanks to my family for their support, and to my staff for their help.

Author's Note

Gujarati cuisine has proved to the world that vegetarian food can be both delicious and complex in flavour. It effortlessly combines the sweet, sour, and spicy to create a range of exceptional dishes.

While wheat, rice, millet (*bajra*), and sorghum (*jowar*) are the staples of Gujarati cuisine, ingredients like, groundnut, gram flour, yogurt, lime juice, and sugar or jaggery are the hallmarks of its flavours and textures. The range of spices used varies in terms of flavour, colour and aroma: from the nuttiness of cumin, pungency of asafoetida, and heat from chillies to the vibrant colour and earthy taste of turmeric. The spices may be dried or fresh, whole or ground, or fried in oil to intensify their flavours. A pinch of sugar or jaggery is often added to *dals* and vegetables to balance the flavours and ostensibly to counteract the natural saltiness of Gujarat's water.

Gujarati methods of cooking cover the entire gamut of cooking techniques from the deep-fried to the steamed, affording a delightful mélange of tastes and textures all on one *thali* or platter, all courses being served at the same time in separate *vati* (small bowls).

A traditional meal consists of, rice or *rotli*, *dal* or *kadhi*, a few vegetables (*shaak*), pulses (*kathol*), salad, a pickle, chutney or relish, one or more of Gujarat's famed *farsan* - an extensive collection of any-time delicious snacks and dessert.

While the eating patterns are more or less the same, there are 4 distinct cooking styles in Gujarat, based largely on geographical and climatic conditions: Kathiawar, Surat, Ahmedabad and Kutch. The food of Kathiawar which is a part of Saurashtra, is distinguished by its chilli-hot, often garlicky flavours and a generous use of oil. Cereals like *jowar* and *bajra* grow in abundance in this region and naturally play a major role in the diet.

Surti food on the other hand is milder, with fewer spices and less oil. Vegetables and fruit grow in plenty in the well-watered region providing a variety of fresh produce for the table. It is also a simpler form of cooking, where fresh ingredients are lightly spiced and flash-cooked to retain their flavours and freshness. *Undhiyu* is the one dish that all Surtis are most proud of – a mélange of winter vegetables and spices traditionally cooked in an earthen pot buried under a wood fire.

Ahmedabadi food is understandably more cosmopolitan, given its status as the capital of Gujarat. Its food has a distinct sweetness, which perhaps is responsible for the mistaken impression that all Gujarati food is sweet. Street food and *farsan* come into its own in this busy metropolis, with *dhokla*, *khandvi*, *bhajiya* etc. always available on the go.

Khichdi and *kadhi* are the mainstay of a Kutchi table, with buttermilk playing an important role at every meal. The food is not unlike its Surti counterpart: lightly spiced fresh greens and vegetables, cooked with the minimum oil and just a hint of sweetness. *Osaman* and *puran poli* served with *kadhi* are Kutchi favourites.

This collection of recipes is my way of showcasing the best of Gujarati cuisine, featuring traditional as well more contemporary fare. You will see that cooking Gujarati food is not a time-consuming process. The key to cooking a successful Gujarati dish is to read the recipe very carefully before beginning, to be sure that you have all the ingredients at hand and to use only the best and freshest ingredients.

Sample the vibrant colours that Gujarati food has to offer, and I am sure you will want to make it a part of your daily meals.

Contents

ROTLI & BHAKRI VAGHERE
INDIAN BREADS

BHAAT & PULAV VAGHERE
RICE

FARALI VANGI
FASTING FOODS

MITHAI & ICE CREAM
DESSERTS

Sherbet Vaghere

Drinks

Keri nu Sherbet

mango squash

INGREDIENTS

- 1 litre Alphonso mango juice, strained (approx. 10 mangoes)
- 1 kg (approx.) sugar
- 1 litre water
- 2 tbsp citric acid
- ½ tsp sodium benzoate (optional)
- ½ tsp potassium metabisulphite (optional)

METHOD

Measure the juice with a cup measure. Measure out an equal quantity of sugar. Mix the sugar with water in a pan and bring to a boil. Add citric acid when the sugar has dissolved completely. Cook for 3-4 minutes and remove from heat. Strain the sugar syrup and set aside to cool. Add strained mango pulp and mix well.

If you are using the preservatives, mix the powders in a little mango mixture and add to the rest of the mixture. Fill in glass bottles and store in the refrigerator. Use 3-4 tablespoons of squash mixed with ¾ glass of cold water and ice, to make 1 glass of mango squash.

Makes 20 glasses

Note: For a smooth drink, mix the squash and water with a rod blender before adding the ice.

Kakdi ane Fudina ni Chaas

chilled cucumber and mint cooler

INGREDIENTS

450 gm cucumber, peeled and sliced
Salt to taste
Pepper to taste
2 tbsp lemon juice
2 tsp finely chopped mint leaves
2 cups yogurt
2 cups ice cold water
½ cup chilled water
1 tsp chopped garlic

To garnish

Mint leaves and *jiralu* powder

METHOD

Sprinkle salt over cucumber and set aside for 30 minutes. Rinse the cucumber and pat dry. Place cucumber with the remaining ingredients in a blender and blend till smooth. Season with salt and pepper. Pour into a stainless steel bowl and chill in the refrigerator. Garnish with mint leaves and sprinkle with *jiralu* powder. Pour into juice glasses and serve chilled.

Serves 4-6

Note: *Jiralu* powder is a Gujarati spice mix which includes asafoetida, black salt, chilli, cumin, dried ginger, rock salt and turmeric.

Vaghareli Chaas

spiced buttermilk

INGREDIENTS

1 cup yogurt
2 cups water
1 tsp oil
¼ tsp cumin seeds
5-6 curry leaves
1 tbsp coriander leaves, finely chopped
1 tbsp finely chopped green chilli
1 tbsp finely chopped ginger
Salt to taste

METHOD

Beat the yogurt with a whisk. Add water and continue beating till smooth. For tempering, heat the oil in a small pan and add the cumin seeds. When they splutter, add curry leaves, chopped coriander, chilli and ginger. Pour over beaten buttermilk. Add salt to taste and serve at room temperature.

Makes 4 glasses

Note: You may also add 1 tablespoon of finely chopped mint to the tempering.

Gulab ane Badam nu Dudh

rose and almond milk

INGREDIENTS

3-4 almonds, soaked in water for 30 min.

1 cup chilled milk

1-2 tbsp rose syrup OR

1 tsp rose essence + 2 tbsp sugar

1-2 ice cubes

Sugar to taste

To garnish

Whipped cream, rose petals and slivered almonds

METHOD

Peel the almonds and discard the skin. Place cold milk, almonds, rose syrup, ice cubes and sugar in a blender and blend until frothy. Pour into a tall glass. Pipe the cream on top and sprinkle almonds and rose petals. Serve chilled.

Serves 1

Nariyal Dudh ane Limda nu Pinu

coconut and curry leaf soother

INGREDIENTS

2 cups freshly grated coconut

12-15 fresh curry leaves

½ cup warm water

Black salt to taste

Lemon juice to taste

To garnish

Lemon slices and lemon grass stalks

To serve

Ice cubes

METHOD

Blend together grated coconut, curry leaves and water in a blender until smooth. Pass the mixture through a strainer, squeezing out all the juice. Add black salt and a few drops of lemon juice to taste. Place 3-4 ice cubes in 2 glasses and pour the liquid over. Garnish with lemon slices and provide lemon grass stalks as stirrers. Serve chilled.

Serves 2

Masala Chai Thandi
spiced iced tea punch

INGREDIENTS

4 cups water

8 tsp black tea leaves

2 tsp Tea Masala (page 14)

¾ cup rock sugar, powdered

A handful of lemon grass

A handful of mint leaves

Juice of 2 lemons

To garnish

Lemon slices studded with cloves, slivered ginger, lemon grass stalks, cinnamon sticks, fresh mint leaves and whole cardamoms

To serve

Flavoured ice cubes

METHOD

Bring water to a boil in a pan. Remove from heat and add tea leaves, tea *masala* and sugar. Cover and set aside for 2-3 minutes. Remove lid and add lemon grass and mint leaves. Cool to room temperature. Strain and add lemon juice. Adjust sugar to taste.

Pour the mixture into a large punch bowl. Add all the garnishes to the bowl along with some ice cubes. To serve, place 5-6 ice cubes at the bottom of each glass. Top with chilled tea and serve. Provide straws which can be used as stirrers.

Serves 6

Annanas ane Keri no Rus
pineapple-mango duet

INGREDIENTS

2 cups chopped ripe mango

60 ml rum (optional)

1 tbsp lemon juice

4 cups pineapple juice

To garnish

Slices of tropical fruit such as star fruit, mango or pineapple

To serve

Ice cubes and 6 highball glasses (12 oz size)

METHOD

Pureé mangoes, rum, lemon juice, and ½ cup water in a blender. Pour ¼ cup pureé in each high ball glass. Add 2-3 ice cubes to each glass. Top up with pineapple juice (approx. ⅔ cup). Garnish with fruit slices and serve chilled.

Serves 6

Nariyal Paani nu Pinu

coconut refresher

INGREDIENTS

2 tender coconuts, with their flesh

2 tsp sugar

A small pinch of salt

½ cup finely diced apple, sprinkled with ½ tsp lemon juice

To garnish

Grenadine syrup and a few red rose petals

METHOD

Chill the coconuts in their shells. Remove coconut water and flesh from the shells.

Blend together with sugar in a blender till smooth. Add a pinch of salt. Divide diced apple in 4 glasses and pour coconut water, with a splash of grenadine syrup, decorate with rose petals and serve.

Serves 4

Masala ni Chai

spiced tea

INGREDIENTS

1 cup milk

1 cup water

1 tsp Tea Masala (recipe follows)

3 tsp sugar or to taste

1 cardamom, freshly crushed in shell

2 tsp strong tea leaves

A few lemon grass leaves, chopped (optional)

METHOD

In a stainless steel pan, mix together milk and water and bring to a boil on medium heat. Add tea *masala*, sugar, cardamom and tea leaves. Continue to boil till rich golden in colour. Add lemon grass, turn the heat off, cover and let it stand for 5 minutes. Strain into individual teacups and serve hot.

Makes 2 cups

TEA MASALA

Grind together 10 grams each of black peppercorns, cinnamon, cloves and dried ginger and 40 grams of whole cardamom to a smooth powder. Store in an airtight container.

Farsan & Nasta

Snacks & Starters

Lila Channa na Samosa

green gram pastry triangles

INGREDIENTS

- 250 gm plain flour + 1 tbsp oil for binding the dough
- Water, as required
- 1 tbsp oil
- 6-8 green chillies, coarsely chopped
- 500 gm fresh green gram, *(hara chana)*, coarsely ground
- Salt to taste
- Juice of 2 lemons
- 2 tbsp finely chopped coriander
- Oil for deep-frying

To serve

- Green Chutney (page 48)

METHOD

Mix together the plain flour, oil and water and knead to make a semi-soft dough. Cover and set aside. Heat 1 tablespoon oil in a frying pan and fry the chillies for 2 minutes. Add a little water if the mixture sticks to the bottom of the pan. Cook for 3-4 minutes. Add green gram, salt and a little more water. Cook until gram is tender and the mixture is dry. Stir in lemon juice and chopped coriander. Set aside to cool.

Divide the dough into 8 portions. Shape each portion into a ball. Roll out each ball with a rolling pin to make a 4-5-inch disc. Cut the disc in half. Fold each half to form a cone, and stick the ends using a little water to moisten. Fill the cone with 1 tablespoon of mixture and seal the edges using a little water. Just before serving, deep-fry the *samosas* until crisp. Serve hot with green chutney.

Makes 8 *samosas*

Lila Channa na Samosa
(recipe on adjacent page)

Ghughra (recipe on page 20)

Bajri na Pudla
(recipe on adjacent page)

Bajri Wada (recipe on adjacent page)

Bajri Na Pudla
millet pancake

INGREDIENTS

- 1/4 cup millet, soaked overnight
- 1 cup millet flour
- 1/2 cup yogurt
- 2 tbsp ginger-chilli-garlic paste
- 1 medium onion, diced
- 1 medium tomato, diced
- Salt to taste
- 8-10 (5-inch square) banana leaves
- Oil for frying

To serve

- Green Chutney (page 48) and fried green chillies

METHOD

Cook the millet in a pressure cooker, till the pressure is released once (1 whistle). Mix millet flour and yogurt in a bowl to make a smooth batter. Cover and set aside for 1-2 hours. To the batter, add ginger-chilli-garlic paste, diced onion and tomato, and salt to taste. If you find the batter too thick, add a little water.

Heat a *tawa*; brush it with a little oil. Apply a little oil on banana leaves. Place each leaf on a hot *tawa* and spread 2-3 tablespoons of the prepared batter. Smooth the surface. Sprinkle with millet grains and cover it with another leaf. Cook on a medium heat, turn it over and cook the other side again. Serve hot with green chutney and fried chillies.

Makes 6-8 pancakes

Bajri Wada
millet fritters

INGREDIENTS

- 200 gm millet flour
- 1/4 tsp turmeric powder
- 1/4 tsp chilli powder
- 1 tbsp sesame seeds
- 4 tbsp oil
- 1/2 cup sour yogurt
- Salt to taste
- Oil for frying

METHOD

Mix all the ingredients and knead to make a soft dough. Shape into round coin-sized patties and press in the centre with your thumb to make a depression. Fry in hot oil until brown. Serve as a teatime snack.

Makes 16-18 *wadas*

Ghughra

savoury crescents

INGREDIENTS

For dough

2 cups plain flour

2 tbsp melted ghee

Salt to taste

¼ tsp asafoetida

Oil for deep-frying

For stuffing

2 tbsp oil

½ tsp cumin seeds

¼ tsp asafoetida

2 cups shelled green peas, slightly crushed

2 tbsp beaten rice, soaked in little water

1 tsp ginger-green chilli paste

1½ tsp sugar

4 tbsp grated coconut

2 tsp chopped coriander

1 tsp sesame seeds

1 tbsp lemon juice

Salt to taste

To serve

Date and Tamarind Chutney (page 25)

METHOD

For dough

Sift the flour; add melted ghee, salt, asafoetida and enough water, and knead to make a firm dough. Knead the dough for 5 minutes, cover and set aside.

For stuffing

Heat the oil in a pan; add the cumin seeds and asafoetida and heat till the seeds sizzle. Add the green peas and stir. Sprinkle some water, cover with a lid and cook for a few minutes. Remove the lid and allow the mixture to dry.

Remove the green pea mixture onto a steel plate and allow to cool. Add the soaked beaten rice, ginger-green chilli paste, sugar, grated coconut, coriander, sesame seeds, lemon juice and salt and mix well.

To make ghughra

Divide the dough into 20 equal portions. Roll out each portion into 3-inch disc. Place a spoonful of the stuffing mixture in the centre of each circle. Gently fold the circle into a semicircle and seal the edges.

Twist the edges carefully with the thumb and forefinger. Deep-fry in hot oil over medium heat till golden brown.

Serve hot with date and tamarind chutney or Green Chutney (page 48).

Tip: You can also make the filling with French beans and green peas, fresh green pigeon peas or fresh corn.

Makes 20 *ghughras*

Shaakbhaji no Handvo

savoury vegetable cake

INGREDIENTS

- 1½ cups mixed vegetables (cauliflower, peas and carrots), chopped and boiled
- 2 medium potatoes, cubed and boiled
- ¼ cup gram flour
- 1 cup maize flour
- 1½ cups thick coconut milk
- ½ tsp turmeric powder
- 1 tbsp ginger-chilli paste
- ¼ cup finely chopped coriander
- 2 tsp powdered sugar
- 2 tbsp lemon juice
- Salt to taste
- 1 tbsp fruit salt

For tempering

- 4 tbsp oil
- 2 tsp mustard seeds
- 2 tsp sesame seeds
- 2-3 dried round red chillies
- A few curry leaves

METHOD

Grease an 8 x 10-inch baking dish with oil. Mix all the ingredients except fruit salt in a bowl. When you are ready to bake, add fruit salt to the mixture and pour it into the baking dish.

For tempering, heat oil in a small pan and add mustard and sesame seeds. When they splutter, add chillies and curry leaves. Sprinkle the tempering over the vegetable mixture.

Bake in a hot oven at 240°C/475°F/Gas Mark 9 for 25-30 minutes or until the top is golden. Remove and cool slightly. Cut into small square pieces and serve with tomato sauce or chutney.

Serves 6-8

Masala Meva

spiced mixed roasted nuts

INGREDIENTS

- 100 gm cashew nuts
- 100 gm almonds
- 100 gm peanuts
- 100 gm lotus seeds
- 1-2 tbsp ghee
- 1 tsp salt
- 1 tsp dried mango powder
- 1 tsp coarsely ground black pepper

METHOD

Dry-roast the nuts and lotus seeds and set aside. In a thick-bottomed pan, heat the ghee and add the roasted nuts. Fry for 30 seconds. Add the spices and fry again until the nuts are coated with the spices. Remove from heat and set aside to cool. Fill in an airtight jar.

Makes 2 cups

Cheese ane Papad na Rolls

cheese and lentil crisp rolls

INGREDIENTS

- 4 thin *moong papads*
- 250 gm processed cheese, cut into 1-inch sticks
- Oil for deep-frying
- 1 tsp chilli powder

METHOD

Place *papad* on a worktop and sprinkle enough water to soften it. Cut each one into 1-inch strips. Place one cheese stick at the edge of each *papad* strip and roll it up lightly. Secure the ends with a toothpick. Holding one end of the toothpick, deep-fry in hot oil. Remove and drain on absorbent paper. Sprinkle chilli powder. Repeat for remaining *papads*.

Serves 6

Mixed Chevda
crisp party mix

INGREDIENTS

- 2-3 tbsp oil
- ½ cup peanuts
- ½ cup roasted Bengal gram
- ½ cup split Bengal gram
- 100 gm small fried *papad*
- 100 gm potato straws
- 100 gm lotus seeds, roasted
- 100 gm sago, soaked and fried
- 100 gm wafers
- 100 gm rice wafers, fried
- 100 gm sliced coconut, roasted
- 100 gm popcorn
- 1 tbsp *chaat masala*
- 1 tbsp chilli powder
- 1 tbsp dried mango powder
- 1 tsp black salt
- 1 tsp cumin powder
- 1 tsp sesame seeds
- Salt to taste
- Sugar to taste

METHOD

Heat the oil in a wide pan and add peanuts and both varieties of gram. Fry for 2-3 minutes. Mix together all the spices in a small bowl. Add the remaining ingredients to the pan one by one with the spice mixture, salt and sugar. Remove from heat and set aside to cool. Store in an airtight jar.

Makes approx. 1 kg

Baked Ragda-Pattice

baked potato patties with white pea sauce

INGREDIENTS

For ragda

- 250 gm dried white peas (*vatana*), soaked overnight
- A pinch of soda bicarbonate
- 2-3 tbsp oil
- 1 medium onion, finely chopped
- 1 medium tomato, finely chopped
- 1-2 bay leaves
- ½ tsp mustard seeds
- ½ tsp turmeric powder
- ½ tsp chilli powder
- 1 tbsp ginger-chilli paste
- A few curry leaves
- Salt to taste
- 2 tbsp tamarind pulp
- 1 tbsp jaggery
- ½ tsp dried mango powder

Masala for ragda (to be roasted in 1 tbsp oil and powdered)

- 4 (1-inch) cinnamon sticks
- 4 cardamoms
- 4 cloves
- 5-6 dried round red chillies
- 5-6 slices dried coconut
- ½ tsp sesame seeds
- ½ tsp cumin seeds
- ½ tsp coriander seeds
- ½ tsp aniseed
- 1 tsp peppercorns
- 1 tsp poppy seeds

For potato pattice

- 1 kg potatoes, boiled, peeled and mashed
- 2 slices bread, soaked in water
- Salt to taste
- 2 tbsp finely chopped coriander
- Juice of 1 lemon
- ½ cup Date and Tamarind Chutney (recipe follows)

For potato piping

- 1 large potato, boiled, peeled and mashed
- 1-2 tsp butter
- 1-2 tsp cornflour
- Salt to taste
- Pepper to taste
- 1-2 tsp milk

To garnish

- Slices of onions, capsicum and tomatoes

To serve

- Green Chutney (page 48) or tomato ketchup

METHOD

For ragda

Cook the peas with soda bicarbonate in a pressure cooker till soft. Set aside. Heat oil in a pan and sauté onion until soft. Add the tomato and bay leaves. Add mustard seeds, powdered *masala*, turmeric and chilli powders, ginger-chilli paste and curry leaves. Fry for 3-4 minutes. Add boiled peas along with the water they were boiled in, salt, tamarind pulp, jaggery and mango powder.

Bring to a boil and simmer till the gravy gets thick. Remove from heat and set aside.

For potato pattice

Mix together mashed potato with soaked and mashed bread slices, salt, chopped coriander and lemon juice. Make a smooth mixture by mixing with your palms. Divide the mixture into two parts and set aside.

For potato piping

Mash the potato and add butter, cornflour, salt, pepper, and milk. Fill this in a piping bag. Add extra milk if the mixture feels too dry to pipe.

To assemble

Grease an 8x10-inch baking dish with oil, and layer half the potato pattice mixture at the bottom. Spread the cooked *ragda* over the potato evenly. Spread date and tamarind chutney and cover with remaining potato mixture. Apply a little oil if the mixture sticks to your hand while spreading. Arrange sliced onions, capsicum and tomatoes on top. Pipe the potato mixture to form a uniform design. Drizzle a little milk and bake in a preheated oven until the top turns golden brown (approx. 20-25 minutes). Remove and let it cool for 5 minutes. Cut into square pieces and serve hot with green chutney or tomato ketchup.

Serves 8-10

DATE AND TAMARIND CHUTNEY

Cook 200 gm seedless dates and a walnut-sized ball of tamarind, 2 cups of water, salt and chilli powder to taste in a pressure cooker till the pressure is released 2-3 times (2-3 whistles). Cool. Process the mixture in a blender until smooth and pass through a strainer. If you find the chutney a little thin, boil for 5-10 minutes until thick. Use as required.

Makes 1½ cups

Khatta Dhokla

steamed sour rice and lentil cakes

INGREDIENTS

2 cups *dhokla atta*

½ tsp fenugreek seeds

½ tsp sugar

3 cups sour yogurt, at room temperature

2 tbsp ginger-chilli paste

2 tbsp oil + for greasing

Juice of 1 lemon

2 tsp fruit salt

Salt to taste

Dhokla steamer (*dhokadia*) with small stainless steel *thali*

To garnish

Chilli powder Or black pepper powder

To serve

Green Chutney (page 48)

METHOD

Mix together *dhokla atta*, fenugreek seeds, sugar and yogurt and soak overnight to ferment and rise. Next morning add ginger-chilli paste, mix well and check if the batter is of dropping consistency; if not add a little warm water to thin it.

Boil water in the steamer. Grease the *thali*, with oil. Divide the batter in 2 parts. When the water starts to boil, mix together half the lemon juice, 1 tablespoon of oil, 1 tablespoon of hot water and 1 teaspoon of fruit salt.

As soon as it starts frothing, fold it gently into one half of the batter. Pour the batter into 2-3 greased plates depending on the thickness required. Sprinkle chilli powder or pepper powder over the batter.

Steam covered for 7-8 minutes. Remove and set aside for 5 minutes. Cut into square pieces. Repeat with remaining batter. Serve hot with green chutney.

Serves 6-8

Khatta Dhokla
(recipe on adjacent page)

Tawa no Handvo
(recipe on page 30)

Khandvi (recipe on adjacent page)

Khandvi

gram flour rolls

INGREDIENTS

- 1 cup gram flour, sieved
- 2 cups thin buttermilk
- ½ tsp turmeric powder
- ¼ tsp asafoetida
- 1 tbsp ginger-chilli paste
- Salt to taste
- Oil for greasing

For tempering

- 1 tbsp oil
- ½ tsp mustard seeds
- ½ tsp sesame seeds
- A pinch of asafoetida
- 4-5 curry leaves
- 2-3 green chillies, chopped

To garnish

Finely chopped coriander and grated coconut

METHOD

Mix together all the ingredients with gram flour and prepare a smooth batter. Place the batter in a container that fits in the pressure cooker and cook till the pressure is released 7 times (7 whistles). Remove the container when the pressure drops.

Mix the batter with a rounded spoon to make it smooth. Grease 4-5 stainless steel plates with a little oil. Spoon approximately ½ cup of mixture on each plate and spread it very thinly. Allow it to cool completely. Starting from the edge, roll up like a Swiss roll. Cut each roll into 1½-inch pieces and arrange them on a plate.

For tempering

Heat oil in a small pan; add mustard and sesame seeds. When they splutter, add asafoetida, curry leaves and chillies. Add 1 tablespoon water and sprinkle the mixture over the *khandvi* rolls. Garnish with coriander and coconut. Serve at room temperature or cold.

Makes 24 rolls

Tawa no Handvo

pan-fried savoury cake

INGREDIENTS

- 2 cups Handva Atta (recipe follows)
- 1 cup sour yogurt
- 1 tsp sugar
- 1 cup grated bottle gourd (see note below)
- Salt to taste
- 2-3 tsp ginger-chilli paste
- ½ tsp soda bicarbonate
- A pinch of asafoetida
- 2 tbsp oil + for greasing
- 1 tsp fruit salt
- 1 tsp lemon juice

For tempering

- 4-5 tbsp oil
- 1 tsp mustard seeds
- 2 tsp sesame seeds
- A pinch of asafoetida
- 3-4 dried round red chillies
- A few curry leaves

To serve

- Green Chutney (page 48) or sweet and sour pickle

METHOD

Soak *handva atta* with sour yogurt and sugar for 6 hours or overnight. Add grated bottle gourd, salt, ginger-chilli paste, soda bicarbonate, asafoetida, 2 tablespoons oil and the fruit salt mixed with a little lemon juice and mix well. Place in the refrigerator. In a small pan, heat 4 tablespoons oil; add mustard and sesame seeds. When they splutter, add asafoetida, red chillies and curry leaves.

Heat a small frying pan; coat it with a little oil. Pour ½ cup of prepared batter into the hot pan and spread evenly. Cover with a lid and cook for 2 minutes. Flip the cake with a flat spoon. Pour 1 tablespoon of tempering, and spread evenly. Cover and cook again until golden. Remove from pan, cut into wedges and serve with green chutney or sweet-sour pickle.

Serves 6-8

Note: You can use shredded cabbage, boiled corn or green peas, or chopped mixed boiled vegetables in place of bottle gourd.

HANDVA ATTA

- 1 cup skinless split green gram
- 1 cup rice
- ½ cup split Bengal gram
- ¼ cup wheat

Grind together all the ingredients to make a coarse flour.

Makes 3 cups

Bhakharvadi

crisp spiced rolls

INGREDIENTS

For dough

500 gm plain flour

100 gm gram flour

Salt to taste

¼ cup oil + for deep-frying

For filling

500 gm potatoes, boiled and mashed

1 tbsp *garam masala*

3 tbsp fresh coriander, chopped

1 tbsp ginger-chilli paste

1 tsp chilli powder

2 tbsp grated dried coconut

2 tbsp sesame seeds, toasted

100 gm gram flour vermicelli (*sev*)

Juice of ½ lemon

METHOD

Mix together both the flours and salt. Add the oil and then add enough water to make a semi-soft dough. Divide the dough into 3 portions and set aside.

Mix all the ingredients for the filling and divide into 3 parts. Roll out 1 part of the dough into a large *rotli*. Spread one part of the mixture evenly all over the surface and roll it up tightly. Cut into 1-inch pieces. Set aside for ½ hour. Deep-fry the pieces in hot oil until crisp and golden. Drain and serve hot.

Makes 20-24 *bhakharvadis*

Kutchi Daabeli

kutchi-style bread and potato snack

INGREDIENTS

¼ cup oil

2 tbsp *daabeli masala*

2 medium tomatoes, grated

3-4 medium potatoes, boiled, peeled, and mashed

Salt to taste

Masala peanuts

1 tsp oil

⅓ cup roasted and peeled peanuts

1-2 tbsp *daabeli masala*

To assemble daabeli

Garlic Chutney (recipe follows)

8 *ladi pav*, split in half

Chopped coriander leaves, as required

Finely chopped onion, as required

METHOD

In a frying pan, heat oil and sauté *daabeli masala*. Add grated tomato and when cooked add mashed potato. Cook for 5 minutes. Add salt to taste.

For masala peanuts

Heat the oil in a frying pan and add the *daabeli masala* and peanuts, and cook for 2 minutes.

To assemble daabeli

Spread garlic chutney on the bottom half of the *pav*, and spread with the potato mixture. Sprinkle coriander, *masala* peanuts, and chopped onions. Press the top half of the *pav* on top and serve.

Makes 8 *daabelis*

Note: You can use any type of *masala* peanuts for this dish.

GARLIC CHUTNEY

Soak 50 dried red chillies (*bedki* variety) in water and drain. Clean ½ cup garlic cloves and make a paste using a mortar and pestle. Add 3 teaspoon salt and 1 teaspoon cumin seeds. Grind to a fine paste with the help of a little oil. Store in an airtight container.

Makes ½ cup

Hariyali Chaat
spicy green salad snack

INGREDIENTS

1 tbsp oil
1/2 tsp cumin seeds
1-2 green chillies, slit
4-5 curry leaves
250 gm green gram
250 gm shelled green peas
A pinch of soda bicarbonate
Black salt to taste
Salt to taste
1 tbsp dried mango powder
1/4 cup Mint Chutney (page 43)
1 medium tomato, finely chopped
1 medium onion, finely chopped
1 tbsp finely chopped coriander
1 tbsp green chillies
Lemon juice to taste

To garnish

100 gm spinach *sev*

To serve

12 potato baskets OR
tart cases

METHOD

Heat oil in a pan; fry cumin seeds, chillies and curry leaves. Add the gram and peas with a pinch of soda bicarbonate. Sprinkle a little water to avoid sticking. Cook, uncovered, until soft. Add black salt, salt and mango powder. Mix well.

Just before serving, mix in the mint chutney, tomato, onion, coriander, lemon juice, and chopped green chillies. Spoon the mixture into tart cases or potato baskets, garnish with spinach *sev* and serve.

Makes 12 appetiser portions

Makai na Rolls

corn rolls

INGREDIENTS

- 1 tbsp oil
- ½ medium capsicum, finely chopped
- 1 medium onion, grated
- 2 tbsp ginger-chilli-garlic paste
- 1 tbsp *garam masala*
- Salt to taste
- 2 cups corn kernels, coarsely ground
- 1 tsp lemon juice
- 1 tbsp finely chopped coriander
- 1 tbsp cornflour
- Breadcrumbs as required
- Oil for shallow-frying

To serve

- Mint Chutney (page 43)

METHOD

Heat the oil in a frying pan, and sauté capsicum, onion and ginger-chilli-garlic paste for 2-3 minutes. Add *garam masala*, salt and corn. Cook until soft. Remove from heat and add lemon juice, coriander and cornflour.

Shape the mixture into cylindrical kebabs. Roll them in breadcrumbs and shallow-fry them in oil, in a non-stick frying pan, until golden brown. Serve hot with mint chutney.

Makes 10-12 rolls

Khaman Dhokla

steamed gram flour cakes

INGREDIENTS

1 cup gram flour, sieved
1½ tbsp semolina
3 tbsp oil + for greasing
Salt to taste
3 tsp sugar
¾ cup water
½ tsp citric acid
Juice of ½ lemon
1 tsp fruit salt
1 tsp soda bicarbonate

For tempering

2 tbsp oil
½ tsp mustard seeds
½ tsp sesame seeds
A pinch of asafoetida
2-3 green chillies, chopped
4-5 curry leaves
¼ cup water

To garnish

3-4 tbsp finely chopped coriander and grated coconut

METHOD

Mix both the flours. Add 2 tablespoons of oil, salt, sugar and half the water. Set aside. Boil water in a wide pan with a metal ring at the bottom. Grease a 9-inch stainless steel plate with a rim with oil and place it on the ring.

In a small bowl mix together remaining water, citric acid, 1 tablespoon oil, fruit salt, soda bicarbonate, and lemon juice, and add this to the flour mixture.

Mix the batter lightly in a circular movement. Pour immediately onto the greased plate.

Cover tightly and steam for 15 minutes. Remove from the pan and set aside to cool slightly.

For tempering

Heat the oil in a small pan; add mustard and sesame seeds. When they splutter, add asafoetida, green chillies and curry leaves. Allow the spices to splutter for 1 minute. Add water to the tempering and pour over steamed *dhokla*. Garnish with coriander and coconut. Serve hot.

Serves 4-6

Paneer-Vatana ni Puri

cottage cheese and green pea puffs

INGREDIENTS

- 2 tsp + 2 tbsp oil
- 500 gm green peas, shelled and crushed
- 2-3 green chillies, chopped
- 100 gm cottage cheese, crumbled
- 2 tbsp coriander leaves, finely chopped
- 1 tsp *garam masala*
- Salt to taste
- 1 cup wholewheat flour
- 1 tbsp plain flour
- Oil for deep-frying

To serve

- Green Garlic Chutney (recipe follows)

METHOD

In 2 teaspoons oil, fry the peas for 5 minutes till they dry out slightly. Remove from the heat and add green chillies, cottage cheese, coriander, *garam masala* and salt. Set aside. Add 2 tablespoons oil and salt to wholewheat flour and plain flour, and make a soft dough. Cover and set aside for ½ hour. Divide this dough into 10-12 small balls. Spread each ball with your hands to make a 2-inch disc. Place 1 tablespoon of pea mixture in the centre, and bring the edges together to seal the filling. Roll out lightly. Deep-fry in hot oil or brush with a little oil and bake in a hot oven for 10-15 minutes. Serve with green garlic chutney.

Serves 6

GREEN GARLIC CHUTNEY

Mix together 1 cup of chopped coriander with 2-3 chopped green chillies, 1-inch piece ginger, 4 tablespoon green garlic with leaves. Grind all together and add juice of 1 lemon, 1 teaspoon sugar, and salt to taste.

Makes 1 cup

Methi na Bhajia

fenugreek fritters

INGREDIENTS

1 cup gram flour

2 tbsp rice flour

2 tbsp wholewheat flour

2 medium-sized ripe bananas, peeled and mashed

1½ cups fresh fenugreek leaves, washed and roughly chopped

2 tbsp ginger-chilli paste

Salt to taste

2 tbsp oil + for deep-frying

A pinch of soda bicarbonate

To serve

Green Chutney (page 48)

METHOD

Mix all the flours and mashed banana in a bowl. Add enough water to make a thick batter. Add chopped fenugreek leaves, ginger-chilli paste and salt. Mix well.

Cover and set aside for 5-6 hours. When ready to serve, heat the oil for frying. Heat 2 tablespoons of oil and add to the batter along with soda bicarbonate. Shape tablespoons of the mixture into dumplings and drop into the hot oil. Put one dumpling in first to check if the oil is hot enough. Deep-fry the dumplings in batches. Serve hot with green chutney.

Serves 6

Palak Sev-Puri

spinach crisps and gram noodle snack

INGREDIENTS

15-20 spinach leaves, washed and cut into 2-inch circles

Oil for frying

2 medium potatoes, cubed and boiled

1 small onion, finely chopped

½ cup Sweet and Sour Chutney (page 43)

½ cup Garlic Chutney (page 32)

½ cup fine *sev*

For batter

¼ cup gram flour

¼ cup water

½ tsp salt

½ tsp chilli powder

½ tsp lemon juice

½ tsp carom seeds

A pinch of asafoetida

A pinch of fruit salt

METHOD

Mix all the ingredients for the batter and beat until smooth. Set aside for 30 minutes. Drain spinach leaves and dip each one in the prepared batter and fry in hot oil, 2-3 at a time, until crisp. Drain on absorbent paper.

Arrange the fried spinach on a plate. Place 3-4 potato cubes on each one. Sprinkle chopped onion, and top with both chutneys to taste. Sprinkle *sev* and coriander leaves and serve at once.

Serves 4

Shaak na Mould

vegetable moulds

INGREDIENTS

2 medium carrots, grated
½ cup breadcrumbs

For potato mixture

8 large potatoes, boiled and mashed
¼ cup sago, soaked for ½ hour
1 tbsp toasted and ground peanuts
1 tbsp ginger-chilli paste
2 tbsp lemon juice
Salt to taste

For green pea mixture

2 tbsp oil
A pinch of asafoetida
1½ cups shelled green peas, crushed
A pinch of soda bicarbonate
2 tbsp coriander leaves
2 tbsp grated coconut
1 tbsp lemon juice
1 tbsp ginger-chilli paste
1 tsp *garam masala*
Salt to taste

To serve

Green Chutney (page 48) or tomato sauce

METHOD

Spread grated carrot at the bottom of an 8-inch greased ring mould tin. Sprinkle breadcrumbs all over.

For potato mixture

Divide mashed potato into two-third and one-third parts. Take two-third of the mashed potato and mix with the drained sago. Add the remaining ingredients and mix well. Press some of this mixture on the bottom and sides of the mould. Set aside a little mixture for the covering.

For green pea mixture

In a small pan, heat oil and add asafoetida. Add the peas and soda bicarbonate. Cook until soft. Remove from heat and set aside to cool. Add the reserved one-third mashed potato and the remaining ingredients and mix well. Layer this mixture over the potatoes. Top it with the potato mixture that was set aside. Bake in the oven at 400°F/200°C/Gas Mark 6 for 20 minutes. Remove and cool slightly. Unmould and serve hot with green chutney or tomato sauce.

Serves 8-10

Bhaaji na Muthia
green vegetable dumplings

INGREDIENTS

1 cup wholewheat flour
¼ cup millet flour
¼ cup sorghum flour
1 tbsp semolina
1 tbsp gram flour
2 cups fenugreek, spinach and any other leafy greens
2 tbsp ginger-chilli paste
2 tbsp oil
2 tbsp yogurt
1 tsp sugar
1 tsp sesame seeds
1 tsp salt
A pinch of soda bicarbonate

For tempering

1-2 tbsp oil
½ tsp mustard seeds
½ tsp sesame seeds
½ tsp asafoetida
A few curry leaves

To garnish

Grated fresh coconut and chopped coriander

To serve

Green Chutney (page 48)

METHOD

In a large bowl, mix together all the flours. Add the remaining ingredients and mix to make a very soft dough. Divide the dough into 2 or 3 parts and shape into rolls. Place them in a greased perforated steamer tray. Cover and steam the rolls for 30 minutes. Remove and set aside to cool. Cut the rolls into ½-inch slices.

Heat the oil for tempering in a frying pan. Add mustard and sesame seeds and when they splutter add asafoetida and curry leaves. Arrange the sliced dumplings over the tempering and heat them through. Turn over and cook the other sides as well. Transfer to a serving plate, garnish with grated coconut and chopped coriander. Serve hot with green chutney.

Serves 6

Bharela Dahiwada

stuffed lentil dumplings in yogurt

INGREDIENTS

2 cups skinless split black gram, soaked for 6-7 hours

Salt to taste

Oil for deep-frying

For stuffing

1 tbsp oil

¼ kg French beans, finely chopped

¼ kg shelled green peas, slightly crushed

A pinch of soda bicarbonate

Salt to taste

1 tbsp ginger-chilli paste

To serve

Dahiwada masala (a mixture of salt, chilli powder and roasted cumin seed powder.)

Thick beaten yogurt

Date and Tamarind Chutney (page 25)

METHOD

Grind the split black gram with a little water, to make a smooth paste. Beat the paste well, with a round spoon. Drop a small ball of this mixture into a bowl of water, if it floats then the paste has been beaten adequately.

For stuffing

Heat the oil in a frying pan; add the vegetables with soda bicarbonate, salt and ginger-chilli paste. Cook until soft. Remove from heat and set aside.

Place a wet cloth on a work surface, and drop a dollop of *dal* mixture onto it and press gently to make a 2-inch disc. Spoon the vegetable mixture into the centre and fold over to make a crescent-shaped *wada* with the help of cloth. Heat the oil and fry on medium heat until golden.

Mix *dahiwada masala* in beaten yogurt and pour over fried *wadas* and serve with date and tamarind chutney.

Makes 24 *dahiwadas*

Pawa no Chevdo

spicy roasted beaten rice snack

INGREDIENTS

¼ kg thin beaten rice
¼ cup peanuts
¼ cup roasted gram
1 tbsp oil
1 tsp sesame seeds
1 tsp aniseed
A pinch of asafoetida
A few curry leaves
2 green chillies, slit
Salt to taste
½ tsp turmeric powder
1 tsp powdered sugar
1 cup potato straws

METHOD

Sun-dry the beaten rice for 2-4 hours. Roast the beaten rice and set aside. Deep-fry peanuts and roasted gram.

In a small pan, heat oil and add sesame seeds, aniseed, asafoetida, curry leaves, and green chillies and fry for a few seconds. Add beaten rice, salt, and turmeric powder, and mix well. Once it cools, add the powdered sugar, peanuts, roasted gram and potato straws, and mix again. Store in an airtight tin.

Makes 500 gm

Makai Bhel

spicy corn snack

INGREDIENTS

2 cups boiled corn kernels
1 cup boiled peas
1 cup boiled and cubed potatoes
2 medium onions, chopped
2 medium tomatoes, chopped
1 medium green capsicum, chopped
1 medium unripe mango, chopped
Salt to taste
Chilli powder to taste
Chaat masala to taste
½ cup finely chopped coriander
½ cup Sweet and Sour Chutney (recipe follows)
½ cup Mint Chutney (recipe follows)

To garnish

Fine *sev*, *boondi* and chopped coriander

METHOD

In a large bowl, mix together corn, peas, potatoes, onions, tomatoes, capsicum and mango. Toss gently to mix. Set aside. Just before serving, add salt, chilli powder, *chaat masala*, coriander and chutneys to taste. Serve in individual bowls garnished with *sev*, *boondi* and chopped coriander. Provide additional chutney if required.

Serves 4-6

SWEET AND SOUR CHUTNEY

Mix together in a pan, ½ cup tamarind pulp, ¾ cup jaggery, ½ teaspoon black salt, ½ teaspoon salt and ½ teaspoon pepper powder, 1 teaspoon cumin powder and 1 teaspoon chilli powder. Bring to a boil and set aside to cool.

Makes ¾ cup

MINT CHUTNEY

Blend together to a smooth paste: 1 cup mint leaves, ½ cup coriander leaves, juice of 1 lemon, 1 teaspoon ginger-chilli paste, 1 tablespoon grated coconut, 1 garlic clove (optional), salt and sugar to taste, and a little cold water. Refrigerate.

Makes 1 cup

Handvo
savoury cake

INGREDIENTS

2 cups Handva Atta (page 30)
1 cup sour yogurt
½ tsp soda bicarbonate
2-3 tbsp oil + for greasing
1 cup grated bottle gourd
Salt to taste
2-3 tsp ginger-chilli paste
1 tsp sugar
A pinch of asafoetida
1 tsp fruit salt

For tempering

4-5 tbsp oil
1 tsp mustard seeds
2 tsp sesame seeds
A pinch of asafoetida
3-4 dried round red chillies
A few curry leaves

To serve

Green Chutney (page 48) or sweet-sour pickle and buttermilk

METHOD

Mix together the *handva atta*, sour yogurt and soda bicarbonate and set aside for 6 hours or overnight.

Grease a 6 cup-sized baking dish with a little oil. Preheat the oven to 180°C/350°F/ Gas Mark 4. To the fermented batter, add grated bottle gourd, salt, ginger-chilli paste, sugar, asafoetida, 2 tablespoons of oil and fruit salt mixed with a little water.

Mix the batter very lightly and pour it into the greased baking dish. Place in the freezer till you get the tempering ready.

For tempering

Heat 4 tablespoons of oil in a small pan, add mustard and sesame seeds. When they splutter, add asafoetida, red chillies and curry leaves.

Remove the *handva* from the freezer and pour the tempering over the surface and bake for 20-25 minutes or until golden on top. Remove from the oven and cool. Cut into squares and serve with green chutney or sweet-sour pickle, accompanied by buttermilk.

Serves 6-8

Note: You can use shredded cabbage, corn or boiled green peas in place of bottle gourd.

Handvo (recipe on adjacent page)

Makai Bhel (recipe on page 43)

Bajri Khichu (recipe on adjacent page)

Panki (recipe on page 48)

Bajri Khichu

steamed millet snack

INGREDIENTS

1 tbsp oil
½ tsp cumin seeds
¼ tsp asafoetida
3-4 green chillies, chopped
1 cup water
½ cup millet flour
¼ tsp potassium carbonate
Salt to taste

To serve

Pickle oil

METHOD

Heat the oil in a heavy-bottomed pan; add cumin seeds. When they change colour, add asafoetida and green chillies. Fry for 30 seconds. Add water and bring to a boil. Add millet flour, potassium carbonate and salt at once. Stir vigorously and continuously until there are no lumps and the mixture is thick. Transfer this mixture to a pressure cooker container with water underneath.

Cook till the pressure is released once (1 whistle). Remove from heat and allow to cool slightly. Open the cooker and remove the *khichu*. Apply a little oil on your palms and shape into small round discs with a dent in the centre. Place pickle oil in the centre and serve.

Serves 6

Panki

rice pancakes steamed in banana leaves

INGREDIENTS

For panki

- $1\frac{1}{2}$ cups rice flour
- 2 cups sour yogurt
- $\frac{1}{2}$ tsp sugar
- $\frac{1}{2}$ tsp fenugreek seeds
- 1 tsp green chilli-ginger paste
- Salt to taste
- 6-8 banana leaves, cut into 12-inch squares
- Oil for cooking

To serve

Green Chutney (recipe follows) and Vagharela Marcha (page 67)

For green chutney

- 2 cups coriander leaves, washed and roughly chopped
- 2-3 green chillies, chopped
- 1-inch ginger
- $\frac{1}{2}$ tsp cumin seeds
- 1 tsp sugar
- 1 tbsp roasted split Bengal gram
- Juice of 1 lemon
- A pinch of asafoetida

METHOD

For panki

Place the rice flour in a large bowl; add yogurt, sugar and fenugreek seeds. Mix thoroughly to make a smooth batter. Cover and set aside in a warm place overnight to ferment. The batter should taste sour. Add chilli-ginger paste and salt to the batter and mix thoroughly.

Grease the banana leaves with a little oil. Heat a frying pan or *dosa tawa* and brush with a little oil. Place a greased leaf on it and pour 3-4 tablespoons of batter on the leaf and spread evenly. Cover with another leaf, greased side down and cover with deep metal pan. Let the *panki* cook for 3-4 minutes till set and small bubbles appear. Turn over and cook the other side as well. Serve hot straight from the banana leaf onto the plate, along with green chutney and green chillies.

Serves 6-8

GREEN CHUTNEY

Grind together all the ingredients with a little water to make a smooth paste. Store in the refrigerator.

Makes 1 cup

Bajri-Methi Khakhra ane Paneer

thin millet and fenugreek crisps with crumbled cottage cheese

INGREDIENTS

For methi khakhra

1 cup finely chopped fresh fenugreek leaves

1 tsp sesame seeds

1 tsp carom seeds

Salt to taste

¼ tsp chilli powder

¼ tsp turmeric powder

1 tsp oil

1 cup wholewheat flour

1 cup millet flour

2 tsp ghee

For crumbled cottage cheese

1 tsp salt

1 cup yogurt

1 litre milk

1 tbsp finely chopped tomato

1 tbsp onion

1 tbsp coriander leaves

METHOD

For khakhra

To the fenugreek leaves, add sesame seeds, carom seeds, salt, chilli powder, turmeric powder and oil and set aside for 5 minutes. Add both flours to the mixture with just enough water and mix to make a soft dough. Divide the dough into 15 portions and roll out each portion into very thin discs with the help of little flour. Heat a *tawa* and cook the *khakhra* lightly for a few seconds on both sides. Brush a little ghee on each *khakhra* and roast, pressing down with a cloth, until crisp. Cool and store in an airtight container. Serve with crumbled cottage cheese.

Makes 15 *khakras*

For crumbled cottage cheese

Add salt to the yogurt. Heat milk in a pan and when it comes to a boil, add the yogurt and take off the heat. Cover the pan and set aside for 10 minutes. Strain the mixture through a piece of muslin and place a weight on it to allow all the water to drain out. Remove the cottage cheese from the muslin and place in a bowl. Beat it with a spoon till smooth. Add tomato, onion, coriander and salt if required. Serve at room temperature with *khakhra* or wholewheat toast.

Makes approx. 1 cup

Bajri-Methi ni Puri

millet and fenugreek crisps

INGREDIENTS

½ cup fresh fenugreek leaves, chopped
Salt to taste
1 cup millet flour
1 tsp oil + for deep frying
1 tsp black pepper powder
1 tsp crushed garlic cloves
1 tsp sesame seeds
1 tsp ginger-chilli paste
½ tsp turmeric powder
A little flour

METHOD

Sprinkle ½ teaspoon salt on chopped fenugreek and set aside. Mix together millet flour, 1 teaspoon oil, salt, pepper powder, crushed garlic, sesame seeds, ginger-chilli paste and turmeric powder. Mix fenugreek leaves with the flour mixture and make a semi-soft dough with water. Divide the dough into small cherry-sized balls. Place each ball on a floured surface and with the help of your palms shape into large coin-sized *puri*. Prick with a fork and deep-fry in hot oil over a medium heat, till crisp.

Alternatively, place on a greased oven tray and bake in a preheated oven at 150°C/300°F/Gas Mark 2, for 15 minutes.

Store in airtight container when cool. Serve with chutney or yogurt as a teatime snack.

Makes 18-20 *puris*

Kand na Pudla

yam pancakes

INGREDIENTS

500 gm grated purple yam
250 gm potatoes, peeled and grated
2 tbsp peanuts, coarsely powdered
4 tbsp semolina
2-3 green chillies, chopped
1-inch ginger, grated
2 tbsp coriander leaves, chopped
2 tbsp grated coconut
1-2 tbsp yogurt
Salt to taste
Oil for deep-frying

To serve

Green Chutney (page 48)

METHOD

In a large bowl, mix together all the ingredients except oil. Whisk vigorously with a rounded spoon.

Heat the oil in a frying pan. Drop 1-2 tablespoonfuls of the mixture to form small pancakes, 2-3 at a time. Cook on both sides and serve hot with green chutney.

Serves 4-6

Makai Cutlet Chaat

corn cutlet chaat

INGREDIENTS

For cutlets

½ cup boiled and crushed corn
1 cup mashed potato
1 tbsp ginger-chilli paste
1 tbsp finely chopped coriander
1 tbsp mint leaves
2 tbsp cornflour
2 tbsp lemon juice
½ tsp *garam masala*
Salt to taste
Sugar to taste
Oil for shallow-frying

For chaat

1 tbsp oil
1 tsp cumin seeds
2 green chillies, finely chopped
2 cups beaten yogurt
Salt to taste
Chilli powder to taste
Chaat masala to taste

To garnish

Sev, fresh pomegranate kernels and chopped coriander

METHOD

For cutlets

Mix all the ingredients together and make 10 round flat cutlets. Shallow-fry in oil, 2-3 pieces at a time. Keep warm.

For chaat

Heat oil in a small pan; add cumin seeds and green chillies and sauté for a few seconds. Mix this into beaten yogurt. Add salt, chilli powder and *chaat masala*. Mix well.

To assemble and serve

Pinch each cutlet in 2-3 places and place them on a serving plate or 1 on individual serving plates. Pour prepared yogurt evenly to cover the cutlet. Sprinkle *sev*, pomegranate kernels and coriander to garnish. Serve immediately.

Sprinkle additional chilli powder and *chaat masala* to taste.

Serves 6

Amiri Khaman

crumbled gram flour cakes with a rich tempering

INGREDIENTS

200 gm *khaman dhokla* mix OR
250 gm ready-made *khaman dhokla*
1 tbsp sugar
1 tbsp lemon juice

For tempering

3 tbsp oil
1 tsp mustard seeds
1 tsp sesame seeds
½ tsp asafoetida
6-8 garlic cloves, crushed
2-3 green chillies, chopped
A few curry leaves
3 tbsp broken cashew nuts
3 tbsp raisins

To garnish

Grated coconut, chopped coriander and fine *sev*

METHOD

Prepare *dhokla* according to the directions on the packet. Set aside to cool. Crumble the *dhokla* with your fingers. Add sugar and lemon juice, mix well and set aside.

Heat the oil in a pan; add mustard and sesame seeds and when they splutter, add asafoetida, garlic, chillies and curry leaves. Fry for a few seconds and add cashew nuts and raisins. Cook until golden. Add the fried ingredients to the crumbled *dhokla* and mix well. Transfer to a serving bowl and garnish with coconut, coriander and *sev*. Serve warm.

~ Serves 4

Lila Mug na Bhajia

green gram fritters

INGREDIENTS

¼ kg split green gram

3 green chillies, chopped

2 garlic cloves, crushed

3 tbsp chopped coriander

Salt to taste

2 onions, chopped

1 tsp toasted sesame seeds

Oil for deep-frying

To serve

Green Chutney (page 48)

METHOD

Soak the green gram in water for at least 4 hours. Grind along with chillies, garlic and coriander, to make a thick paste. Add salt. Just before frying the *bhajia* add finely chopped onions, sesame seeds and mix well. Heat the oil in a *kadai*. Take two spoonfuls of the mixture on your palm, flatten it with your fingers and place in the hot oil. Deep-fry 8-10 at a time on medium heat in very hot oil. Serve hot with green chutney.

Makes approx. 24 *bhajias*

Kand na Rolls

Spiced Yam Rolls

INGREDIENTS

2 kg purple yam

¼ kg peanuts OR
Roasted Bengal gram, crushed

100 gm arrowroot flour

1 tbsp *garam masala*

1 tbsp sesame seeds, roasted

Juice of 2 lemons

2 tsp sugar

Salt to taste

¼ tsp asafoetida

1 tbsp ginger and chilli paste

To garnish

Fresh grated coconut and finely chopped coriander

METHOD

Peel the yam, cut in large chunks and boil in a pan or pressure cooker until soft. Cool, peel and mash till smooth. Add remaining ingredients.

Shape into small 2-inch rolls and deep-fry. Serve hot, garnished with grated coconut and chopped coriander.

Makes 14-16 rolls

Lila Mug na Bhajia
(recipe on adjacent page)

Amiri Khaman (recipe on page 53)

Mug na Dhokla
(recipe on adjacent page)

Mug na Dhokla
steamed green gram cakes

INGREDIENTS

1 cup whole green gram, soaked for 6 hours

1 tbsp coriander leaves, finely chopped

1 tbsp oil + for greasing

1 tbsp ginger-chilli paste

Salt to taste

1 tsp fruit salt

Juice of ½ lemon

For tempering

2 tbsp oil

½ tsp mustard seeds

A pinch of asafoetida

4-5 curry leaves

To garnish

3-4 tbsp finely chopped coriander and grated coconut

To serve

Green Chutney (page 48)

METHOD

Grind together the green gram, coriander leaves, and water to a coarse batter of medium consistency. Heat a large pan with enough water and place a metal ring at the bottom of the pan. Grease a stainless steel plate with a rim (*thali*) with oil, and place it on the ring in boiling water.

For the *dhokla* mixture, mix together green gram batter, ginger-chilli paste, salt, 1 tablespoon of oil, and fruit salt mixed with lemon juice. Mix the batter lightly in a circular motion, till all the ingredients are well incorporated. Pour this into the greased plate over hot water immediately. Cover tightly and steam for 15 minutes. Remove from the pan and set aside to cool slightly.

For tempering

Heat the oil in a small pan and add mustard seeds. When they splutter add asafoetida and curry leaves. Pour this over the steamed *dhokla*. Garnish with coriander and coconut. Serve hot with green chutney.

Serves 4-6

Ugela Mug na Dahiwada

sprouted green gram dumplings in yogurt

INGREDIENTS

- ½ cup split green gram, soaked for 6 hours
- ½ cup skinless split black gram, soaked for 6 hours
- Salt to taste
- 2 tbsp ginger-chilli paste
- 1 large potato, boiled and mashed
- 1 cup sprouted green gram, boiled
- ½ tsp *garam masala*
- ½ tsp chilli powder
- 1 tsp sugar
- Juice of ½ lemon
- Oil for deep-frying

To serve

2 cups beaten yogurt, fine *sev*, Date and Tamarind Chutney (page 25), salt, roasted cumin and chilli powders, and 2 tablespoons finely chopped coriander

METHOD

Mix both varieties of gram and grind to a fine paste without adding much water. Add salt and ginger-chilli paste. Set aside. Mix mashed potato with boiled green gram. Add *garam masala*, chilli powder, salt, sugar and lemon juice and mix well. Shape the mixture into walnut-sized balls.

Heat oil to smoking in a *kadai*. Dip potato and gram balls into the gram mixture to coat thickly. Fry in hot oil until golden. Remove from oil and drop the balls into a bowl of water. Soak for 5-7 minutes. Drain and remove from water and place on a serving platter. Top the *wadas* with beaten yogurt. Garnish with fine *sev*, date and tamarind chutney, salt, cumin powder, chilli powder, and coriander. Serve cold.

Serves 6-8

Damni Dhokla

steamed spiced multi-grain cakes

INGREDIENTS

2 cups *damni dhokla* flour

2 cups sour yogurt

1/4 cup water

2 tbsp peanut or sesame oil

1/4 tsp asafoetida

1/4 tsp chilli powder

1/4 tsp turmeric powder

1 tsp salt

1 tbsp green chilli-ginger paste

1 tsp fruit salt

1/4 cup brown chickpeas, soaked overnight and boiled

12-15 leaf cups made with thick green leaves

To serve

Green Chutney (page 48)

METHOD

In a large bowl, mix together the flour, yogurt, water, oil, asafoetida, chilli powder, and turmeric powder, and salt. Cover and place in a closed oven or cupboard overnight to ferment.

Boil 8-10 cups of water in a steamer. Place a perforated plate over the boiling water and cover with the lid.

Add green chilli-ginger paste along with fruit salt and a little water to the fermented flour mixture. Pour 1/2 cup of mixture into each leaf cup and sprinkle 5-6 boiled chickpeas on top.

Place the leaf cups so they stand upright in the steamer and steam for 20-25 minutes. Remove and serve hot with green chutney.

Makes 12-14 *dhoklas*

Note: *Damni dhokla* flour is a mixture of rice, *dals* and spices, which is commercially available.

Makai Wada ane Puri Chaat

corn dumplings on crisps

INGREDIENTS

For wada

1 cup corn kernels, boiled and crushed

½ cup potatoes, boiled and mashed

2 tbsp thick sour yogurt

½ cup gram flour

2 tbsp finely chopped coriander

2 tbsp grated coconut

1 tsp ginger-chilli paste

½ tsp *garam masala*

1 tsp dried mango powder

Oil for deep-frying

To serve

20 crisp 1-inch *puris*, Sweet and Sour Chutney (page 43), Green Chutney (page 48), 100 gm *sev* and freshly chopped coriander

METHOD

Place all the ingredients for the *wada* in a large bowl and mix well. Shape the mixture into 1-inch *wada* and deep-fry in oil. Place the *puris* in a serving plate, apply a little sweet and sour chutney on each *puri*. Place a *wada* on each *puri* and dot it with green chutney, sprinkle a little *sev* and coriander, and serve.

Serves 6-8

Kand no Handvo

savoury yam pie

INGREDIENTS

1 kg purple yam, boiled and mashed

2 potatoes, boiled and mashed

2-3 tbsp thick yogurt

Salt to taste

Juice of 1 lemon

2 tbsp oil

2 tbsp green chilli-ginger paste

2 cups shelled green peas, boiled and crushed

Sugar to taste

4 tbsp freshly grated coconut

4 tbsp coriander leaves, freshly chopped

For tempering

2 tbsp oil

1 tsp mustard seeds

1 tsp sesame seeds

4-5 dried round red chillies

A few curry leaves

To garnish

Freshly grated coconut and freshly chopped coriander

To serve

Green Chutney (page 48) OR Coconut Sauce (recipe follows)

METHOD

Mix together mashed yam, potatoes, yogurt, salt and lemon juice. Set aside. In a frying pan, heat 2 tablespoons of oil; fry chilli-ginger paste for a few seconds. Add green peas, sugar, salt and remaining lemon juice. Remove from heat; add coconut and coriander. Leave to cool.

Spread half the yam and potato mixture in an 8x10-inch rectangular or 9-inch square greased baking dish. Spread a layer of the pea mixture evenly. Cover with a layer of yam and then the remaining pea mixture over the yam. Smooth the top with your palms.

For tempering

Heat oil in a small pan; add mustard and sesame seeds, and when they splutter, add chillies and curry leaves. Spread the spice mixture over the yam mixture evenly. Bake in a hot oven at 180°C/350°F/Gas Mark 4, for 15-20 minutes. Let it rest for 4-5 minutes, then sprinkle with grated coconut and coriander, and cut into 1-inch squares. Serve hot with green chutney or coconut sauce.

Serves 6-8

COCONUT SAUCE

Heat 1 teaspoon oil; add a pinch of cumin seeds and 4-5 curry leaves. Add this to 1 cup of coconut milk. Add salt and sugar to taste. Serve warm or cold.

Makes 1 cup

Makai na Dhokla

steamed corn cakes

INGREDIENTS

1 cup grated fresh corn cooked in a little milk

1/2 cup thick yogurt + 1/2 cup water

1 1/2 cups *khaman dhokla* mix

Salt to taste

8 green chillies + 1-inch ginger, ground to a paste

A pinch of asafoetida

1 tbsp hot oil + 1 tsp oil

1 1/2 tsp *dhokla* mix powder from the sachet

A little oil for greasing

For tempering

2 tbsp oil

1 tsp mustard seeds

1 tsp cumin seeds

5-6 dried round red chillies

4 green chillies, finely chopped

A pinch of asafoetida

A few curry leaves

To garnish

Finely chopped coriander and grated coconut

To serve

Green Chutney (page 48)

METHOD

In a large bowl, mix together cooked corn, yogurt and water mixture along with the *khaman dhokla* mix. The batter should be of a thick pouring consistency. Add salt, chilli-ginger paste, asafoetida and 1 tablespoon of hot oil and mix well. Cover and keep for 15-20 minutes.

Boil sufficient water in a large pan and place a metal ring in the water-filled pan.

Grease a stainless steel plate with a rim (*thali*), with 1 teaspoon oil and place it on the brass ring. Mix *dholka* mix flavouring powder with 1/4 cup of water and add this to the *dhokla* batter and immediately pour the *dhokla* mixture into the *thali* and cover with a larger *thali*. Steam for 20 minutes.

Remove from the steamer and sprinkle 1 cup of water over it, let it cool.

For tempering

Heat the oil in a small pan. Add mustard seeds, cumin seeds, round chillies, chopped green chillies, asafoetida, and curry leaves. Fry for 1 minute and sprinkle over the cooled *dhokla*, garnish with coriander and coconut and serve with green chutney.

Serves 6-8

Batata na Dhokla

steamed potato cakes

INGREDIENTS

- 1/4 kg coarsely ground gram flour
- 2 tbsp oil
- 1/2 kg potatoes, boiled and mashed
- 4 tbsp semolina
- 1/4 tsp asafoetida
- 2 tbsp ginger-chilli paste
- 1/4 kg yogurt
- Salt to taste
- 1/4 tsp soda bicarbonate
- 1/4 kg green peas, boiled

To garnish

Grated coconut and finely chopped coriander

To serve

Green Chutney (page 48)

METHOD

Mix gram flour with 1 tablespoon oil and add to mashed potato. Add semolina, asafoetida, ginger-chilli paste and yogurt. Mix well, cover and set aside for 2 hours.

Before you begin to make the *dhokla*, bring water to a boil in a large pan. Place a ring in the pan. Grease a stainless steel plate with a rim (*thali*) with 1 tablespoon of oil and place it on the ring. Heat 1/4 cup of water and add salt and soda bicarbonate and immediately, add this to the potato mixture along with the boiled peas. Pour this mixture onto the greased plate, cover and steam the *dhokla* for about 10-15 minutes.

Cut into square pieces, garnish and serve hot with green chutney.

Serves 4-6

Ponk na Dhokla

steamed fresh green millet cakes

INGREDIENTS

1 cup fresh green millet, steamed and slightly crushed

2 cups ready-made *dhokla* batter OR

1 cup *dhokla atta* } Mixed and fermented overnight
1¼ cups sour yogurt
½ tsp fenugreek seeds

2 tbsp chopped ginger-chilli mixture

Salt to taste

½ tsp soda bicarbonate

½ tsp fruit salt

Oil for greasing

For tempering

2 tsp oil

1 tsp mustard seeds

½ tsp asafoetida

2-3 dried round red chillies

A few curry leaves

To serve

Green Garlic Chutney (page 36)

METHOD

Mix crushed green millet with the *dhokla* batter. Add chopped ginger-chilli mixture and salt. If using ready-made batter, mix the powder in the sachet with a little water; or mix soda bicarbonate and fruit salt in a little water and add to the batter. Divide the batter into 2 parts. Grease two 8-inch round stainless steel plates with a rim (*thali*), with oil. Boil the water in a steamer and place a ring in the pan.

Pour the batter into the prepared plates and steam for 10-15 minutes. Remove from steamer, cool for 5 minutes, and cut into small squares. Heat the oil for tempering in a small pan; add mustard seeds and when they splutter, add asafoetida, chillies and curry leaves. Remove from heat and sprinkle over *dhokla*. Serve with green garlic chutney.

Serves 6-8

Trevati Dal na Dhokla

steamed three-lentil cakes

INGREDIENTS

- ½ cup skinless split green gram
- ½ cup skinless split black gram
- ½ cup split Bengal gram

(Soak for 6-8 hours, 1 day prior to requirement)

- 3 tbsp sour yogurt
- 1 tbsp sugar
- Oil for greasing
- 1 tbsp ginger-chilli paste
- Salt to taste
- 2 tbsp oil
- 2 tbsp lemon juice
- 1 tsp soda bicarbonate
- 1 tsp fruit salt

For tempering

- 2 tbsp oil
- 1 tsp mustard seeds
- A pinch of asafoetida
- A few curry leaves

To garnish

Finely chopped coriander and freshly grated coconut

To serve

Green Chutney (page 48)

METHOD

Grind the soaked gram to a thick paste. Place the paste in a large bowl and add sour yogurt and sugar. Mix well. Add enough warm water to make a batter of dropping consistency. Cover and set aside to ferment for 6-8 hours.

Heat a large pan with enough water and place a metal ring at the bottom of the pan. Cover and allow water to boil. Grease a round stainless steel plate with oil and place it on the ring. Lightly mix the fermented batter. Add ginger-chilli paste, salt and 2 tablespoons oil. In a small bowl, mix together lemon juice with soda bicarbonate and fruit salt. Fold this liquid into the batter and gently mix. Pour this mixture into the greased plate immediately. Cover and steam for 30-35 minutes. To check if the *dhokla* is done, insert a knife through it, if it comes out clean, the *dhokla* is ready. Remove from heat and set aside.

For tempering

Heat the oil in a small pan; add mustard seeds. When they splutter, add asafoetida and curry leaves. Remove from heat and sprinkle this over steamed *dhokla*. Garnish with coriander and coconut and serve hot or warm with green chutney.

Makes 30-35 *dhoklas*

Kobi na Muthia

cabbage dumplings

INGREDIENTS

1 cup wholewheat flour
½ cup gram flour
1 tbsp oil
Salt to taste
½ tsp sugar
¼ tsp soda bicarbonate
A pinch of asafoetida
200 gm shredded cabbage
1 tbsp ginger-chilli paste
¼ cup yogurt

For tempering

2 tbsp oil
1 tsp mustard seeds
2 tsp sesame seeds
A pinch of asafoetida
2-3 dried round red chillies
A few curry leaves

To garnish

Finely chopped coriander and grated coconut

To serve

Green Chutney (page 48)

METHOD

Sprinkle a little salt over the cabbage and set aside for 10 minutes. Mix both the flours and add, oil, salt, sugar, soda bicarbonate and asafoetida. Add the cabbage, ginger-chilli paste, and yogurt to the flour mixture and mix well. Add some more oil if required and knead to make a dough. Divide the dough into 2 portions.

Shape small portions of the dough into rolls and place on an oiled sieve and steam for 15-20 minutes. Remove from the sieve and cool. Slice into 1-inch thick slices.

For tempering

Heat the oil in a frying pan; add mustard seeds, when they splutter, add sesame seeds and asafoetida. Finally, add chillies and curry leaves. Add steamed *muthia* to the tempering and mix very gently to coat all the pieces with the spices. Fry until slightly crisp. Garnish with coriander and coconut and serve with green chutney.

Serves 4-6

Methi Dhokla
steamed fenugreek cakes

INGREDIENTS

250 gm packet *khaman dhokla* mix
½ cup fenugreek leaves
2 tsp ginger-chilli paste
1 tbsp oil
1½ cups water
Oil for greasing
Small *idli* moulds

To serve

Coconut chutney

METHOD

Mix together the *dhokla* mix, fenugreek leaves, ginger-chilli paste, the small sachet which comes with the packet, oil and 1½ cups of water.

Spoon the mixture into the greased *idli* moulds. Steam in a covered pan over hot water for 15 minutes. Remove with a sharp knife and serve hot with coconut chutney.

Makes 30 small *dhoklas*

Vagharela Marcha
tempered green chillies

INGREDIENTS

2 tbsp ghee
A pinch of asafoetida
100 gm green chillies with stem, washed and slit vertically
1 tsp black salt
1 tsp dried mango powder
1 tsp roasted cumin powder
Juice of 1 lemon
Salt to taste

METHOD

Heat ghee in a small pan till it smokes; add asafoetida and chillies. Cook until chillies are slightly soft. Add the remaining ingredients and cook for 3-4 minutes. Ensure that the spices don't burn. Remove from heat and cool. Serve as an accompaniment to any savoury dish.

Makes ½ cup

Dal Dhokli

wholewheat pasta in lentil gravy

INGREDIENTS

For dal

½ cup split pigeon peas
½ tsp turmeric powder
2 tbsp raw peanuts
1-inch ginger
½ tsp asafoetida
2 tbsp ghee
½ tsp mustard seeds
A few curry leaves
1 tbsp ginger-chilli paste
2 tbsp jaggery
4-5 *kokum* rinds
Salt to taste

For dhokli

½ cup wholewheat flour
1 tbsp gram flour
½ tsp carom seeds
½ tsp turmeric powder
½ tsp red chilli powder
Salt to taste
Warm water to bind the dough, as required

To garnish

Finely chopped coriander

To serve

Finely chopped onions, green chillies and lemon wedges

METHOD

For dal

Wash and soak the split peas in 2 cups water for half an hour. Transfer to a pressure cooker and add turmeric powder, peanuts, ginger and asafoetida, and cook till pressure is released thrice (3 whistles). Remove from heat and cool.

For dhokli

Mix together the flours, carom seeds, turmeric powder, chilli powder and salt, and a little warm water, and knead to make a soft dough. Cover and set aside for half an hour. Divide the dough into 6-8 portions. Dust a board and roll each one out into 7-inch discs. Place the discs separately, on paper, so that they don't stick to each other.

For dal dhokli

Lightly mix the cooked *dal* with a wooden spoon. Heat ghee in a large pan; add mustard seeds, and when they splutter, add curry leaves and the cooked *dal* mixture. Add the rest of the ingredients and simmer for 10 minutes. Cut the discs into 1-inch long strips and then cut the strips into diamond-shaped pieces. When the *dal* mixture begins to boil add 2-3 pieces at a time. Make sure each piece remains separate. Cook for 7-8 minutes, till done. Garnish with coriander. Serve immediately, with finely chopped onions, green chillies and lemon wedges.

Serves 6

Kachumber ~ Raita ~ Athana ~ Chutney

Salads ~ Pickles ~ Chutney

Kobi-Gajar-Simla Mirchi nu Kachumber

cabbage-carrot-capsicum salad

INGREDIENTS

250 gm cabbage, thinly grated
250 gm carrots, thinly grated
Salt to taste
1 large capsicum, thinly sliced
Juice of 1 lemon
1 tsp sugar
2-3 tbsp grated coconut
2-3 tbsp finely chopped coriander

For tempering

2 tbsp oil
½ tsp mustard seeds
½ tsp skinless split black gram
2 green chillies, slit
A pinch of asafoetida
A few curry leaves

METHOD

Sprinkle cabbage and carrot with a little salt, and set aside for 15 minutes. Drain excess water. Mix together cabbage, carrot and capsicum in a bowl. Add lemon juice, sugar, coconut and chopped coriander.

For tempering, heat the oil in a small pan; add mustard seeds and split gram. When they splutter add green chillies, asafoetida and curry leaves. Fry for 1 minute. Pour over vegetables. Toss gently to mix. Chill and serve.

Serves 4

Makhana Raita

puffed lotus seed salad

INGREDIENTS

- 50 gm puffed lotus seeds
- 2 cups milk
- 1 tbsp ghee
- 1 tbsp raisins
- 1 tbsp sunflower seeds
- 3 cups yogurt, beaten } Mix together, strain and chill overnight
- ½ cup fresh cream }
- Salt to taste
- Sugar to taste

To garnish

- Finely chopped coriander

METHOD

Discard the hard black flakes from lotus seeds and boil in milk till tender. Strain and set aside. Heat the ghee in a *kadai*; fry the raisins and sunflower seeds. Remove from pan and set aside.

To the chilled yogurt add, cooled lotus seeds, raisins, sunflower seeds, salt and sugar. Mix well. Garnish with chopped coriander and chill. Serve as an accompaniment with *paratha*.

Makes 3 cups

Kacha Papaya nu Shaak

green papaya salad

INGREDIENTS

1 tbsp oil
1 tsp mustard seeds
A pinch of asafoetida
A few curry leaves
3-4 green chillies, slit
1-inch ginger, finely chopped
2 (2-inch pieces) fresh turmeric, peeled and chopped
250 gm unripe green papaya, peeled, halved and sliced
1 tbsp coriander leaves, chopped
Salt to taste
Sugar to taste
Lemon juice to taste

For garnishing

Finely chopped coriander

METHOD

In a small pan, heat oil; add mustard seeds and when they splutter, add asafoetida, curry leaves, chillies, ginger and turmeric. Cook for 3-4 minutes, stirring occasionally.

Add papaya and cook till slightly tender. Add coriander, salt, sugar and lemon juice and mix well. Transfer to a serving bowl, garnish with coriander and serve at room temperature.

Serves 4

Note: You can also use grated papaya instead of slices.

Kacha Papaya nu Shaak
(recipe on adjacent page)

Khaman Kakdi (recipe on page 76)

Top: Methia Keri (recipe on adjacent page)
Right: Suko Sambhar (recipe on page 77)
Left: Keri nu Shaak (recipe on page 78)

Methia Keri

fenugreek-flavoured mango pickle

INGREDIENTS

- 1 kg unripe mangoes, washed and cut into cubes
- ¾ cup rock salt, slightly crushed
- 2 tbsp turmeric powder
- 1 cup split fenugreek seeds
- ¼ cup fenugreek seeds
- 2 tbsp split mustard seeds
- 2 cups red chilli powder
- 1 tsp asafoetida
- ½-¾ cup mustard oil, heated and cooled

METHOD

Rub the mango pieces with a little salt and turmeric powder and set aside for 1-2 hours. Mix all the dry spices together in a bowl. Rub mango pieces with the spice mixture and transfer to a glass jar. Press them down lightly as you fill the jar. Pour cooled oil into the jar to cover the surface.

Cover the jar tightly and store in a cool place. Allow the mangoes to marinate for 8-10 days. Stir the pickle from time to time. If it feels a little dry at any point, you may add a little extra oil. Transfer to smaller jars and use as required.

~ Makes 1½ kg

Khaman Kakdi

cucumber and coconut salad

INGREDIENTS

- 250 gm cucumber, peeled and chopped or grated
- Salt to taste
- 3-4 tbsp grated coconut
- 3-4 green chillies, seeded and chopped
- 3-4 tbsp peanuts OR Roasted Bengal gram, coarsely ground
- 1 tsp sugar
- Juice of 1 lemon

To garnish

- Finely chopped coriander

METHOD

Apply salt to cucumber and set aside for half an hour. Drain the excess water from the cucumber and place it in a bowl. Add the rest of the ingredients. Garnish with chopped coriander and chill until ready to serve.

Serves 4-6

Teliyu

pickled potatoes in mustard oil

INGREDIENTS

- 2 tbsp mustard oil
- 4 tbsp water
- 2 tbsp split mustard seeds, coarsely powdered
- ½ tsp turmeric powder
- 2 tsp rock salt, powdered
- ½ tsp asafoetida
- 500 gm potatoes, boiled, skinned and chopped into large pieces
- 6-8 green chillies, slit and halved

METHOD

In a flat plate, mix together oil, water and split mustard seeds. Rub your palm over these ingredients in a circular movement until they are mixed completely. Add turmeric powder, salt and asafoetida. Add the potatoes and chillies and toss to mix. Set aside for 1 hour or more. The potatoes will pickle in the mustard mixture. Use this as a pickle. Store in airtight jar in the refrigerator.

Serves 6

Suko Sambhar

pickle spice mix

INGREDIENTS

1 cup split mustard seeds

1 tbsp split fenugreek seeds

⅓ cup turmeric powder

4-5 tbsp asafoetida

2 cups rock salt, slightly crushed

3 cups Reshampatti chilli powder

½ litre (approx.) mustard oil

METHOD

In a large bowl, mix together split mustard and fenugreek seeds. Add turmeric powder, asafoetida, salt and chilli powder one by one, mixing well after each addition until all the spices have been added. When the spices are properly incorporated, add oil, a little by little. When you are able to shape the mixture into a ball, that's when you know it has absorbed enough oil. This recipe requires approximately ½ litre oil.

Transfer the mixture to a glass jar and store in a cool dry place. Use as required for mango pickle, to spice up a dish, or as an accompaniment to a meal.

Makes 6½ cups

Keri nu Shaak

sweet and spicy mango pickle

INGREDIENTS

1 cup unripe mango, peeled and chopped into ½-inch pieces

1 tsp salt

½ tsp turmeric powder

1 cup jaggery, chopped

1 tsp red chilli powder

For tempering

1 tsp oil

½ tsp mustard seeds

½ tsp fenugreek seeds

½ tsp asafoetida

2-3 dried round red chillies

METHOD

To the mango pieces, apply salt and turmeric powder and set aside for half an hour or till the mango releases some water. Drain and remove from bowl.

For tempering, heat oil in a medium-sized thick-bottomed pan. Add mustard and fenugreek seeds. When they splutter add asafoetida and chillies along with mango pieces. Cook, stirring, on a low heat till the mango softens slightly.

Add jaggery and keep stirring until the jaggery melts and the gravy thickens slightly. Remove from heat and add chilli powder. Set aside to cool. When completely cool and thick, transfer to an airtight jar and store in a cool place.

Makes approx. 250 gm pickle

Bharela Marcha nu Athanu

stuffed chilli pickle

INGREDIENTS

- ⅓ cup oil
- ½ cup split mustard grains, ground
- ½ cup rock salt, powdered
- ½ tsp asafoetida
- 1 tsp turmeric powder
- Juice of 1 lemon
- 250 gm thick Bhavnagri green chillies, slit, deseeded and stem removed

METHOD

Mix all the ingredients, except the chillies with half the oil. Stuff chillies with this mixture and transfer them to a glass jar. Pour remaining oil over the chillies.

Toss the chillies very lightly. Place the jar in a cool, dry place. The pickle takes three days to mature.

~ Makes 2 cups

Chhundo

sweet shredded mango pickle

INGREDIENTS

3 large Rajapuri mangoes, grated

⅓ cup rock salt, crushed

Sugar 1½ times the quantity of grated mango, coarsely ground

3 tbsp cumin seeds, slightly crushed

2 tbsp red chilli powder

A pinch of asafoetida (optional)

METHOD

Mix together grated mango and salt. Set aside for half an hour. Squeeze the mangoes lightly, to drain out excess water. In a large bowl, mix together mango and sugar. Cover and set aside overnight.

The next day, remove the lid and cover the bowl by tying a piece of muslin over the mouth of the bowl, and place it in the sun for 3-4 days. Stir every evening to mix well. At the end of the fourth day if the syrup has attained a 2-string consistency, the pickle is done. If not place it in the sun for one more day. Add cumin seeds, chilli powder and asafoetida. Cover and place in the shade for one more day. Next day, transfer the pickle to a large air-tight jar and store in a cool dry place.

Makes 1½-2 kg

Gol Keri

mango pickle with jaggery

INGREDIENTS

- 6 large unripe mangoes, peeled and cut into cubes
- 3 tbsp salt
- 2 tsp turmeric powder
- 1½ cups red chilli powder
- 1 cup split mustard seeds
- 2 tbsp split fenugreek seeds
- 3 tsp asafoetida
- 6 cups chopped jaggery

METHOD

Toss mango pieces with salt and turmeric powder. Spread them on a piece of cloth to dry.

Next day, mix the remaining ingredients, and mango pieces in a large bowl. Toss gently to mix. Fill this in a wide mouth glass jar and cover with a piece of muslin. Store in a cupboard, in a cool place (not in the kitchen). Stir with a clean spoon once in 2 days. The pickle is ready when the jaggery has melted and mango pieces are slightly softened. Transfer 250 gm at a time into a small jar for everyday use.

Makes approx. 5 kg

Limbu nu Athanu

spicy lemon pickle

INGREDIENTS

25 large lemons
100 gm green chillies
100 gm ginger
100 gm red chilli powder
2 tbsp turmeric powder
2 tbsp split mustard seeds
100 gm sugar
½ kg salt
Juice of 5 lemons

For tempering

1 tbsp oil
1 tsp mustard seeds
1 tsp asafoetida

METHOD

Wash and drop lemons in boiling water. Take them out immediately. Drain and cut each lemon into 8 pieces. Wash and chop green chillies and ginger into ½-inch pieces. Mix together chilli powder, turmeric powder, split mustard seeds, sugar and salt in a bowl. Take a clean glass jar and layer lemon pieces, chillies, ginger and dry spices.

For tempering

Heat oil in a pan, add mustard seeds and when they splutter, add asafoetida. Take it off the heat and add this to the lemon mixture. Mix well. Cover and set aside for 3-4 days to marinate. Use as required.

Makes 1½ kg

Murabba
sweet mango pickle

INGREDIENTS

4 cups mango pieces, peeled and boiled in water

5 cups sugar

1 tsp cardamom seeds

1 tsp powdered saffron

METHOD

Mix boiled and drained mango pieces and sugar in a thick-bottomed pan and cook over medium heat. Stir occasionally until syrup attains a 1 thread consistency.

Remove from heat and add cardamom and saffron. Set aside to cool. Fill in a jar and store in a cool dry place.

Makes 1½ kg

Lili Chutney

mango, mint and coriander chutney

INGREDIENTS

2 cups coriander leaves, coarsely chopped

1 cup mint leaves

1/4 kg unripe green mangoes, cut into small pieces

2 tomatoes, cut into small pieces

1 medium onion

7-8 green chillies

1 tbsp sugar

Salt to taste

METHOD

Grind together all the ingredients to make a paste. Add a little water, if necessary. Serve with savoury dishes.

Makes 1 1/2 kg

Shaakbhaaji

Vegetables

Turia-Makai nu Shaak

ridge gourd and corn in spiced coconut sauce

INGREDIENTS

1 tbsp oil
½ tsp cumin seeds
2-3 green chillies, slit
A few curry leaves
500 gm ridge gourd, skinned, slit vertically and cut into 2-inch pieces
A pinch of soda bicarbonate
½ cup corn kernels, boiled
2 tbsp green chilli-ginger paste
1 tsp sugar
2 cups thin coconut milk
1 tsp cornflour
Salt to taste
1 tbsp tamarind water (optional)

To garnish

1 tbsp finely chopped coriander

To serve

Rotlis (page 128)

METHOD

In a heavy-bottomed pan heat oil; add cumin seeds, chillies and curry leaves and fry for a few seconds. Add chopped gourd, soda and a little water. Cook till soft.

Add boiled corn, chilli-ginger paste, sugar and coconut milk mixed with cornflour, and salt to taste. Bring the mixture to a boil, reduce heat and cook till thick. Remove from heat and stir in tamarind water (if using). Garnish with coriander and serve hot with *rotlis*.

Serves 4-6

Note: Make sure you don't over boil the curry or else the coconut milk will curdle.

Dudhi Channa Dal

bottle gourd with split bengal gram

INGREDIENTS

- ½ cup split Bengal gram, soaked in water for 2 hours
- 3 tbsp oil
- ½ tsp mustard seeds
- 1 green chilli, cut into two
- A few curry leaves
- A pinch of asafoetida
- ½ kg bottle gourd, peeled and cut into cubes
- Salt to taste
- 2 medium tomatoes, chopped
- ½ tsp turmeric powder
- ½ tsp coriander-cumin powder
- ½ tsp chilli powder
- ½ tsp *garam masala*
- ½ tsp chopped ginger
- 2-3 *kokum* rinds
- 1 tbsp chopped jaggery

To garnish

- Finely chopped coriander

To serve

- Rotlis (page 128)

METHOD

Boil soaked split gram in water until tender. Heat oil in another pan; add mustard seeds and green chilli. When the seeds splutter, add curry leaves and asafoetida.

Add bottle gourd, salt and a little water. Cover and cook until tender. Add boiled *dal* to gourd along with tomatoes. Add the remaining ingredients and cook till tomatoes are soft and pulpy. Add extra water if required. Garnish with coriander and serve hot with *rotlis*.

Serves 6

Note: You can use cabbage instead of bottle gourd.

Raswala Batata

potatoes in spicy gravy

INGREDIENTS

- ½ kg potatoes
- 3 tbsp oil
- 3-4 dried round red chillies
- ½ tsp mustard seeds
- ½ tsp cumin seeds
- 4-5 cloves
- 4-5 cinnamon sticks
- 2 tbsp peanuts
- 2 tbsp cashew nuts
- ½ tsp dried coriander seeds
- 2-3 bay leaves
- ¼ tsp turmeric powder
- ¼ tsp *garam masala*
- ½ tsp chilli powder
- 2 tbsp tamarind water OR
- Juice of ½ lemon
- Salt to taste

To garnish

- Grated coconut and chopped coriander

METHOD

Peel and cut potatoes into large cubes. Heat oil in a pan; add red chillies, mustard and cumin seeds, cloves and cinnamon. When they splutter and spices are fragrant, add the potatoes, peanuts and cashew nuts.

Add 3-4 cups of water, cover and cook on low heat till almost tender. Add all the remaining ingredients and mix well. Cook for 5-10 minutes. Garnish with grated coconut and coriander.

Serves 4

Batata nu Sukhu Shaak

stir-fried spiced potato

INGREDIENTS

6 tbsp oil

1 tsp cumin seeds

A few curry leaves

1 kg potatoes, boiled, peeled and cut into cubes

Salt to taste

1 tsp coriander-cumin powder

½ tsp turmeric powder

2 green chillies, finely chopped

2 tsp sugar

Juice of 1 lemon

To garnish

¼ cup chopped coriander

To serve

Puris

METHOD

Heat oil in a thick-bottomed *kadai*; add cumin seeds and curry leaves. When the seeds splutter, add the potatoes and salt and mix well. Add all the remaining ingredients and cook until the flavour of the spices has been absorbed.

Garnish with coriander and serve hot with *puris*.

Serves 6-8

Seeng-Batata Chaaswala

drumsticks and potatoes in a buttermilk sauce

INGREDIENTS

1½ cups sour yogurt

½ cup gram flour

½ tsp turmeric powder

1 cup water

3 drumsticks, cut into 2-inch sticks and boiled

3 medium potatoes, boiled, peeled and cut into thick fingers

1 tsp salt

1 tsp jaggery

For tempering

1 tbsp oil

½ tsp mustard seeds

½ tsp cumin seeds

A pinch of asafoetida

2-3 dried round red chillies

A few curry leaves

1 tsp ginger-chilli paste

1 spring onion green stalk, finely chopped

To garnish

Finely chopped coriander

To serve

Rotlis (page 128)

METHOD

Whisk together yogurt, gram flour and turmeric powder with an electric beater. Beat until smooth and all the lumps are removed. Add water and set aside.

For tempering, heat oil in a wide pan; add mustard and cumin seeds. When they splutter add asafoetida, round chillies, curry leaves, ginger-chilli paste and spring onion stalk. Cook until onions are soft. Add drumsticks and potatoes and mix well.

Add the yogurt mixture, salt and jaggery. Bring to a boil, lower heat and simmer for 10-15 minutes or until the gravy is thick. Remove from heat, sprinkle coriander and serve hot with *rotlis*.

Serves 4-6

Seeng-Batata Chaaswala
(recipe on adjacent page)

Dahiwali Fansi
(recipe on adjacent page)

Dahiwali Fansi

french beans in yogurt sauce

INGREDIENTS

½ kg French beans, cleaned and cut into ½-inch pieces

A pinch of soda bicarbonate

3 tbsp oil

½ tsp mustard seeds

¼ tsp asafoetida

2-3 green chillies

Salt to taste

½ tsp chilli powder

1 tsp sugar

2 cups yogurt, beaten

10-12 cashew nuts, halved

A few curry leaves

2 tbsp coriander leaves, finely chopped

METHOD

Place chopped French beans in boiling water with a pinch of soda bicarbonate. Boil for 7-8 minutes. Drain and set aside. In a large frying pan, heat 2 tablespoons oil and add mustard seeds. When they splutter, add asafoetida and green chillies.

Add boiled French beans, salt and chilli powder. Cook until beans are completely soft. Take the pan off the heat and leave to cool completely. Add salt and sugar to the yogurt and add cooled French beans; mix well. Transfer to a serving bowl. In a small *kadai*, heat 1 tablespoon of oil; add cashew nuts and curry leaves and fry for a few seconds. Pour over French beans and sprinkle coriander on top. Chill for 2 hours or until ready to serve.

Serves 4-6

Mixed Palabhaji

spiced mixed greens

INGREDIENTS

- 4 cups amaranth leaves
- 1 cup spinach leaves
- ½ cup dill leaves
- ½ cup Indian sorrel leaves (*khatti bhaji*)
- ½ cup fenugreek leaves
- 4-5 small brinjals
- 2 tbsp oil
- ¼ tsp asafoetida
- 2 green chillies, slit
- Salt to taste

To serve

- Rotlis (page 128)

METHOD

Clean and remove thick veins and stalks from all the leaves before chopping. Finely chop all the leafy vegetables. Wash all the chopped vegetables. Keep the sorrel leaves separate. Chop brinjal into small pieces and soak in water.

Heat oil in a wide pan; add asafoetida and chillies and fry for a few seconds. Add the drained brinjal and all the leafy vegetables, except sorrel leaves. Add ½ cup water and salt. Cover and cook until almost tender. Add the sorrel leaves and cook again for 2 minutes. Serve hot with *rotlis*.

Serves 4

Kanda-Methi nu Shaak

onions with fenugreek leaves

INGREDIENTS

- 3-4 tbsp oil
- 1 green chilli, slit
- 500 gm onions, chopped into small cubes
- 1½ cup fenugreek leaves, roughly chopped
- Salt to taste
- A pinch of soda bicarbonate
- ¼ tsp turmeric powder
- ½ tsp chilli powder
- 1 tbsp jaggery

To serve

Rotlis (page 128)

METHOD

Heat oil in a frying pan; add chilli and onions. Fry till onions are half-cooked. Sprinkle a little water if they stick to the bottom of the pan. Add fenugreek leaves, salt, soda bicarbonate, turmeric and chilli powders. Cook until both vegetables are completely soft. Add jaggery, stir and take off the heat. Serve hot with *rotlis*.

Serves 4-6

Makai nu Shaak

curried corn

INGREDIENTS

- 1½ cups corn kernels
- ¾ cup milk
- 1 tbsp oil
- 1 tsp cumin seeds
- 3-4 green chillies, finely chopped
- 1-inch ginger, finely chopped
- Salt to taste
- Sugar to taste

To garnish

- 2 tbsp grated coconut
- 2 tbsp chopped coriander leaves

To serve

Tandoori rotis

METHOD

Cook corn in a pressure cooker with milk and 1 cup water till the pressure is released thrice (3 times). Heat oil in a pan and fry cumin seeds. When they splutter, add green chillies and ginger. Cook for 2-3 minutes. Add the corn, salt and sugar along with cooking liquid. Cook gently until heated. Add coconut and coriander and serve hot with *tandoori rotis*.

Serves 4-6

Gathia-Muthia nu Shaak

mixed vegetables with fried spiced crispies

INGREDIENTS

For gathia

- 1/2 cup gram flour
- 1 tsp oil
- 1/2 tsp chilli powder
- 1/4 tsp carom seeds
- A pinch of soda bicarbonate
- Salt to taste
- Oil for deep-frying

For methi muthia

- 1/2 cup wholewheat flour
- 1/2 cup gram flour
- 1/2 cup fenugreek leaves, washed and chopped
- 2 tbsp oil
- 1 tsp sugar
- 1 tsp chilli powder
- 1 tbsp ginger-chilli paste
- 1/4 tsp turmeric powder
- 1/2 tsp *garam masala*
- Salt to taste

For vegetable

- 2 tbsp oil
- 1 tsp mustard seeds
- 1/4 tsp fenugreek seeds
- 1/4 tsp asafoetida
- 5-6 curry leaves
- 2 cups water
- 1/4 tsp turmeric powder
- 1 tsp chilli powder
- 1 tsp coriander-cumin powder
- 1/4 kg bottle gourd
- 2 potatoes, boiled, peeled and cubed
- 1/2 cup green peas
- 100 gm French beans, cut into 1/2-inch long pieces
- 1 tbsp jaggery
- 3-4 *kokum* rinds
- Salt to taste

To garnish

- 3-4 tbsp finely chopped coriander leaves and grated coconut

METHOD

For gathia

Mix together all the ingredients with a little water to make a moderately soft dough. Cover and set aside for half an hour. Remove one-fourth of the dough and with the help of a little water, knead to make it pliable. Roll the dough on a flat surface with both your palms to form thick, spaghetti like long rolls or *gathia*. Cut each one into 2-inch long pieces and deep-fry them in hot oil till crisp, drain and set aside.

For methi muthia

Mix all the ingredients together with a little water in a wide bowl and make a soft dough. With the help of a little oil, shape these into 1 1/2-inch long dumplings. Deep-fry in hot oil, drain and set aside.

For vegetables

Heat oil in a pan; add mustard and fenugreek seeds and when they splutter add asafoetida, curry leaves, and 2 cups of water. When the water begins to boil, add turmeric powder, chilli powder, and coriander-cumin powder. Mix well and add all the vegetables.

Cook until vegetables are soft. Add jaggery and *kokum*. Add ½ cup more water, if necessary. Add salt and bring to a boil. Just before serving add *gathia* and *muthia*. Garnish with coriander and coconut and serve hot.

Serves 4-6

Pandola-Methi nu Shaak

snake gourd with fresh fenugreek leaves

INGREDIENTS

1 kg snake gourd (*pandola*), peeled

A pinch of soda bicarbonate

Salt to taste

2 tbsp oil

1 tsp fenugreek seeds

¼ tsp asafoetida

2 small green chillies, slit

1 cup fenugreek leaves, coarsely chopped

1 small ball of jaggery

To garnish

Freshly grated coconut and finely chopped coriander

To serve

Rotlis (page 128)

METHOD

Cut snake gourd into 4-5-inch long pieces. Cut each piece vertically and remove seeds. Cut each halved piece into 1-inch thick semi circle slices. Mix with soda bicarbonate and salt and set aside for 15 minutes.

Heat oil in a frying pan; add fenugreek seeds, asafoetida and green chillies, and fry for 1 minute. Add chopped snake gourd and a little water. Cook, uncovered, for 5-7 minutes. Add fenugreek leaves and salt. Cook until leaves are soft. Add jaggery just before taking off the heat and stir. Garnish with coriander and coconut. Serve hot with *rotlis*.

Serves 4

Panchkutiu Shaak

five vegetables in a coriander-coconut curry

INGREDIENTS

- 3-4 tbsp oil
- ½ tsp carom seeds
- ½ tsp asafoetida
- ½ kg broad beans, stringed and halved
- ½ tsp soda bicarbonate
- 2 medium potatoes, peeled and cut into cubes
- ½ kg small brinjals, stemmed and cubed
- ½ cup shelled peas
- Salt to taste
- 12-14 Methi Muthia (page 96)

For masala

- 1 cup finely chopped coriander
- 1 cup grated coconut
- ½ tsp turmeric powder
- ½ tsp coriander-cumin powder
- 1 tbsp ginger-chilli paste
- 1 tbsp oil
- 1 tbsp sugar
- Juice of 1 lemon

To serve

- *Parathas*

METHOD

In a wide pan, heat oil and add carom seeds and asafoetida. Add broad beans with soda bicarbonate mixed in little water. Cover and cook for 7-8 minutes, until half cooked.

Add potatoes, brinjals and peas along with 1 cup water and salt to taste. In a bowl, mix together all the ingredients for the *masala*. When the vegetables are completely cooked, add the *masala* mixture and 1 cup water and the *muthias*. Cook till all the spices are blended. Serve hot with *parathas*.

Serves 6-8

Bhinda-Batata na Sambharia

ladies' fingers and potatoes with a coconut spice mix

INGREDIENTS

½ cup coriander leaves, finely chopped

½ cup coconut, grated

3-4 tbsp peanuts, roasted and powdered

1 tsp sugar

Salt to taste

Juice of ½ lemon

1 tbsp ginger-chilli paste

2 tbsp ghee

1 tsp cumin seeds

2 medium potatoes, peeled and cut into 3-inch long slices

1 kg ladies' fingers, slit vertically and cut into 3-inch long pieces

To serve

Rajgara na Thepla (page 155) and yogurt

METHOD

Mix together coriander, coconut, peanuts, sugar, salt, lemon juice and ginger-chilli paste. This mixture is called *sambhar*. Toss lightly to mix and set aside.

In a wide pan heat ghee; add cumin seeds and stir-fry; add potatoes, ladies' fingers and salt. Mix well to coat the vegetables with the tempering. Sprinkle the coriander-coconut mixture and mix very lightly. Cover and cook on low heat for 10-15 minutes. Serve hot with *rajgara na thepla* and yogurt.

Serves 4

Note: You can use the same *sambhar* mixture to cook pointed gourd (*parval).*

Bhinda-Batata na Sambharia
(recipe on adjacent page)

Vatana-Muthia nu Shaak
(recipe on adjacent page)

Vatana-Muthia nu Shaak

green peas with fenugreek-flavoured dumplings

INGREDIENTS

½ kg green peas, shelled
A small pinch of soda bicarbonate
1 cup chopped spinach
½ cup coriander leaves
2-3 green chillies
1-inch ginger
Salt to taste
1 tsp sugar
200 gm small Methi Muthia (page 96)

For tempering

2 tbsp oil
½ tsp mustard seeds
A pinch of asafoetida
A few curry leaves

To serve

Fresh coriander, lemon wedges and freshly grated coconut

METHOD

Drop the green peas with a pinch of soda bicarbonate, in boiling water and take them out. Grind together spinach, coriander, chillies, ginger and a little salt, to make a paste.

Heat oil in a pan; add mustard seeds, asafoetida and curry leaves and fry for a few seconds. Add the ground paste and fry for 1 minute. Add peas, sugar, and 1 cup of water and bring to a boil. Just before serving, add the *muthias* and mix. Serve with fresh coriander, lemon wedges and freshly grated coconut.

Serves 6-8

Dahiwala Bhinda

ladies' fingers with yogurt

INGREDIENTS

- 4 tbsp oil
- ½ tsp mustard seeds
- ¼ tsp asafoetida
- A few curry leaves
- ½ kg ladies' fingers, cut into ½-inch pieces
- Salt to taste
- ¼ tsp turmeric powder
- 1 tsp ginger-chilli paste
- 2 cups thick yogurt
- 1 tbsp sugar

To garnish

- Finely chopped coriander

METHOD

Heat oil in a *kadai*; add mustard seeds, when they splutter, add asafoetida and curry leaves. Add ladies' fingers, salt and turmeric powder. Mix well and cook until tender. Make sure the ladies' fingers do not stick to the bottom of the pan. Add ginger-chilli paste and mix well. Remove from heat and cool completely.

Whisk yogurt, a little salt, and sugar together. Pour over cooled ladies' fingers and transfer to a serving bowl. Garnish with coriander and chill until ready to serve.

Serves 4

Turia-Makai nu Shaak

ridge gourd and corn in spiced coconut sauce

INGREDIENTS

1 tbsp oil
½ tsp cumin seeds
2-3 green chillies, slit
A few curry leaves
500 gm ridge gourd, skinned, slit vertically and cut into 2-inch pieces
A pinch of soda bicarbonate
½ cup corn kernels, boiled
2 tbsp green chilli-ginger paste
1 tsp sugar
2 cups thin coconut milk
1 tsp cornflour
Salt to taste
1 tbsp tamarind water (optional)

To garnish

1 tbsp finely chopped coriander

To serve

Rotlis (page 128)

METHOD

In a heavy-bottomed pan heat oil; add cumin seeds, chillies and curry leaves and fry for a few seconds. Add chopped gourd, soda bicarbonate and a little water. Cook till soft.

Add boiled corn, chilli-ginger paste, sugar and coconut milk mixed with cornflour, and salt to taste. Bring the mixture to a boil, reduce heat and cook till thick. Remove from heat and stir in tamarind water (if using). Garnish with coriander and serve hot with *rotlis*.

Serves 4-6

Note: Make sure you don't over boil the curry or else the coconut milk will curdle.

Seeng-Batata na Sambharia

drumsticks and potatoes with coconut spice mix

INGREDIENTS

- 2 drumsticks, cut into 3-inch pieces
- 3 large potatoes, peeled and lengthwise
- ½ cup coriander leaves, finely chopped
- ½ cup coconut, grated
- 3-4 tbsp gram flour, roasted
- ½ tsp turmeric powder
- ½ tsp chilli powder
- 1 tsp sugar
- Salt to taste
- Juice of ½ a lemon
- 1 tbsp ginger-chilli paste
- 2 tbsp oil
- 1 tsp mustard seeds
- A pinch of asafoetida

To serve

Rotlis (page 128)

METHOD

Boil the drumsticks and potatoes separately. Drain and set aside. Mix together chopped coriander, coconut, gram flour, turmeric powder, chilli powder, sugar, salt, lemon juice and ginger-chilli paste. This mixture is called *sambhar*. Toss lightly to mix and set aside.

In a wide pan heat oil; add mustard seeds and asafoetida. When they splutter, add potatoes, drumsticks and salt. Mix well to coat the vegetables with the spices. Sprinkle the coriander-coconut mixture and mix together lightly. Cover and cook on a low heat for 10-15 minutes. Serve hot with *rotlis*.

Serves 4

Note: You can add *sambhar* mixture to ladies' fingers, snake gourd, and ivy gourd.

Fulavar Dahi na Sauce ma

cauliflower in yogurt sauce

INGREDIENTS

1 kg cauliflower

¾ cup milk

1-inch ginger

3 green chillies, ground into paste

¼ cup grated coconut

3 tsp oil

1 tsp skinless split black gram

2-3 cinnamon sticks

2-3 cloves

A pinch of asafoetida

A few curry leaves

2-3 bay leaves

1 cup beaten yogurt

1 tsp salt

To garnish

Finely chopped coriander and grated coconut

To serve

Rotlis (page 128)

METHOD

Chop cauliflower into small pieces. Wash in hot water and place in a pan. Pour milk over it and cook until milk dries up. Grind together the ginger, green chillies and grated coconut.

In another pan, heat oil; add the split gram and fry until pale golden brown. Add cinnamon, cloves, asafoetida, curry leaves and bay leaves.

Add the ground paste and fry for 2-3 minutes. Add yogurt and bring to a boil. Add the cauliflower and salt and mix well. Garnish with coriander and coconut. Serve hot with *rotlis*.

Serves 4-6

Sambharia

stuffed mixed vegetables

INGREDIENTS

250 gm small potatoes, peeled
250 gm small onions, peeled
250 gm small brinjals
100 gm ivy gourd
2 Rajiyani bananas
1 cup gram flour, roasted and mixed with 2 tbsp oil
¾ cup grated coconut
½ cup coriander leaves, finely chopped
1 tbsp coriander-cumin powder
1 tbsp ginger-chilli paste
2 tsp sugar
1 tsp chilli powder
Juice of 1 lemon
Salt to taste

For tempering

6 tbsp oil
2 green chillies, slit
½ tsp mustard seeds
¼ tsp fenugreek seeds
A few curry leaves
¼ tsp asafoetida

To serve

Rotlis (page 128)

METHOD

Make a vertical slit on one side of potatoes and onions. Place in water. Remove the stem from brinjal and make a slit. Cut off both ends of the ivy gourd and slit them vertically. Cut banana into 2-inch long and slit them vertically. Add the rest of the ingredients to the gram flour and mix well. Stuff all the vegetables with this mixture. If there is extra stuffing reserve it to sprinkle on top.

In a large pan, heat oil for tempering. Add chillies, mustard and fenugreek seeds. When they splutter, add curry leaves and asafoetida. Place all the vegetables in the pan except bananas, and mix gently. Cover with a deep metal plate and place water in it. This will help the vegetables to steam, and prevent the vegetables from sticking. Cook on medium heat about 20 minutes till vegetables are half cooked. Remove the lid.

Add stuffed bananas and sprinkle reserved mixture. Continue cooking on medium heat till vegetables are tender. Take off the heat, cover, and set aside. To serve, transfer the vegetables to a deep serving platter and serve hot with *rotlis*.

Serves 6-8

Khatta-Mitha Shaak

sweet and sour vegetable curry

INGREDIENTS

- 2-3 tbsp oil
- 1 tbsp chilli powder
- 1 tsp turmeric powder
- 1 tsp *garam masala*
- 1 tbsp ginger-chilli paste
- 2½ cups water
- 500 gm elephant's foot yam, peeled, cut into cubes, and boiled
- 1 cup shelled peas, boiled
- 2 medium potatoes, boiled, peeled and cubed
- Salt to taste
- 2 tbsp gram flour
- 2 tbsp jaggery
- 2 tbsp tamarind pulp

Grind to a paste

- ¼ cup grated fresh coconut
- 2 tsp poppy seeds
- 6-8 cashew nuts

To garnish

- Finely grated coconut and chopped coriander

To serve

- Rotlis (page 128)

METHOD

Heat oil in a pan and fry the ground paste. Add all the spice powders and ginger-chilli paste and fry for 2 minutes. Add a little water if the mixture is dry. Add the vegetables and salt and mix well.

Mix gram flour with water and add to the vegetable with jaggery and tamarind pulp. Bring to a boil, lower heat and simmer till gravy is thick. Garnish with coconut and coriander and serve hot with *rotlis*.

Serves 6

Undhiyu

surti-style stuffed vegetables

INGREDIENTS

- ½ kg tender *Surti papdi*
- 1 tsp soda bicarbonate
- 100 gm fresh green pigeon peas (*tuvar dana*)
- ¼ kg tender shelled broad beans
- ½ kg round purple yam, peeled and cut into large pieces
- ¼ kg small brinjals, stemmed
- ¼ kg potatoes, peeled
- ¼ kg onions, peeled
- ¼ kg ivy gourd, ends trimmed
- 4-5 small sweet potatoes
- 3 Rajeli bananas
- 1½ cups coriander leaves, finely chopped
- 1½ cups freshly grated coconut
- 4 tbsp finely chopped fresh turmeric
- 4 tbsp finely chopped mango ginger (*amba haldi*)
- 4 tbsp finely chopped ginger
- 1 cup green garlic, finely chopped
- 12 green chillies, finely chopped
- Salt to taste
- Sugar to taste
- Juice of 2 lemons
- 2 tsp *garam masala* (optional)
- 12 Methi Muthia (page 96)
- ½ cup oil
- ½ tsp carom seeds

To garnish

Chopped coriander and grated coconut

To serve

Puris or *parathas*

METHOD

String the *papdi*. Add soda bicarbonate, mix and set aside. Slightly crush the *tuver dana*. Soak all the vegetables in water. Wash the bananas and cut them into halves. Slit all the vegetables at both ends and place them in water till ready to use. For the stuffing, in a large plate, mix together crushed *tuver*, coriander, coconut, fresh turmeric, *amba haldi*, ginger, garlic and chillies. Lightly toss to mix. Add salt, sugar, lemon juice and *garam masala* and mix well. Stuff the potatoes, onions, ivy gourd, sweet potato, brinjals and bananas, reserving some stuffing to be sprinkled on top.

In a large heavy-bottomed pan, heat oil and add carom seeds and the *papdi* along with the *papdi dana*. Cook until soft. Remove from the pan and set aside. In the same oil, place all the stuffed vegetables along with yam in layers. Carefully place them one on top of each other so that stuffing remains intact. Cover and cook until partially cooked. Add the cooked *papdi, muthias* and remaining stuffing. Cover and cook until all the vegetables are very soft. Garnish with coconut and coriander. Serve hot with *puris* or *parathas*.

Serves 8-10

Note: Just before serving or before reheating the vegetables, a little milk is added to enhance the flavour of the spices.

Batata ni Kachri nu Shaak

spiced potato fingers with raisins and cashew nuts

INGREDIENTS

1 kg large potatoes

3 tbsp oil + for deep-frying

1 tsp mustard seeds

2 tbsp sesame seeds

6-8 black peppercorns

$^1/_4$ tsp asafoetida

3-4 dried round red chillies

5-6 curry leaves

2-3 tbsp cashew nuts, broken into pieces

2-3 tbsp raisins

$^1/_2$ tsp turmeric powder

1 tsp chilli powder

1 tsp dried mango powder

Salt to taste

Sugar to taste

To garnish

Finely chopped coriander

To serve

Puris

METHOD

Cut the potatoes into thin finger chips and soak them in cold, salted water for half an hour. Drain and place them on a thick cloth to dry out. Deep-fry in hot oil till crisp, and set aside.

In a wide pan, heat 3 tablespoons oil; add mustard and sesame seeds. When they splutter, add peppercorns, asafoetida, round chillies and curry leaves. Fry for half a minute, add cashew nuts and raisins and fry again.

Finally, add fried potatoes along with turmeric powder, chilli powder, mango powder, salt and sugar to taste. Mix thoroughly. Garnish with coriander and serve with hot *puris*.

Serves 6

Bharela Parval nu Shaak

stuffed gourds

INGREDIENTS

500 gm pointed gourd (*parval*), peeled with the ends removed

½ cup coriander leaves, finely chopped

½ cup coconut, grated

¼ cup peanuts, coarsely ground

2 tbsp ginger-chilli paste

1 tsp sugar

1 tsp garlic, crushed (optional)

Juice of 1 lemon

Salt to taste

For tempering

1 tbsp oil

1 tsp cumin seeds

1-2 green chillies

A few curry leaves

To serve

Rotlis (page 128)

METHOD

Slit the gourds in the middle lengthways without cutting them through. Remove the seeds with a sharp knife, so as to create a hollow space in each one. Set aside.

In a medium bowl, mix together the rest of the ingredients and stuff the gourd with this mixture. Place on a sieve over boiling water and steam them for 15-20 minutes or until soft. Remove from heat and set aside. For tempering, in a frying pan, heat oil, add cumin seeds, chillies and curry leaves. Add steamed gourd and very gently mix so that the gourds don't open up. Cook on a low heat for 5-7 minutes and serve hot with *rotlis*.

Serves 4-6

Dal & Kadhi

Lentils

Khatti-Mitthi Dal

sweet and sour split pigeon pea curry

INGREDIENTS

For dal

1 cup split pigeon peas, washed and soaked

10-12 peanuts

1 tsp ginger-chilli paste

¼ tsp turmeric powder

3-4 *kokum* rinds

2-3 tbsp jaggery

Salt to taste

For tempering

1 tbsp ghee

½ tsp mustard seeds

¼ tsp cumin seeds

¼ tsp fenugreek seeds

3-4 cloves

2 cinnamon sticks

1-2 green chillies

A pinch of asafoetida

6-8 curry leaves

To serve

Steamed rice

METHOD

Pressure-cook the pigeon peas along with peanuts and 4-5 cups of water. When cool, whisk well till smooth. Add the rest of the ingredients for the *dal* and bring to a boil; cook for 10-15 minutes.

For tempering, heat ghee in a pan and add mustard seeds, cumin seeds and fenugreek seeds. When they splutter, add cloves and cinnamon, chillies, asafoetida and curry leaves. Pour the spices over the boiling *dal*. Cook for 5 minutes and serve hot with rice.

Serves 4

Gol Kokum ni Kadhi

sweet and sour kokum-yogurt soup

INGREDIENTS

- $1\frac{1}{2}$ cups sour yogurt
- 4 tbsp gram flour
- 4 cups *dal* water (see note below)
- 3-4 tbsp jaggery
- 3-4 *kokum* rinds
- 2 tsp ginger-chilli paste
- Salt to taste

For tempering

- 2 tbsp ghee
- $\frac{1}{2}$ tsp mustard seeds
- $\frac{1}{2}$ tsp fenugreek seeds
- $\frac{1}{2}$ tsp cumin seeds
- $\frac{1}{2}$ tsp asafoetida
- 3-4 dried round red chillies
- A few curry leaves
- 2 small brinjals, cubed
- 2-inch piece white radish, cut into long strips

To serve

- Steamed rice and Kathan Dal (page 122)

METHOD

In a pan, mix together yogurt and flour with *dal* water whisking well till smooth. Add jaggery, *kokum*, ginger-chilli paste and salt. Bring the mixture to a boil on a medium heat, stirring occasionally. For tempering, in another small pan, heat ghee and add mustard seeds, fenugreek seeds and cumin seeds. When they splutter, add asafoetida, dried chillies and curry leaves.

Add brinjal and radish and cook until vegetables are soft. Add tempering to the yogurt mixture and bring to a boil. Simmer for 15-20 minutes. Serve hot with rice and *kathan dal*.

Serves 6-8

Note: For *dal* water or *dal ka pani*, boil split pigeon peas in water. Drain, reserve the water for cooking. Use the *dal* for *kathan dal*.

Val ni Dal ni Amti

curried field beans

INGREDIENTS

1 large onion, sliced and roasted
1 large piece dried coconut
5-6 garlic cloves, roasted
1 cinnamon stick
3-4 cloves
4-5 black peppercorns
1 tbsp coriander seeds
3 tbsp oil
½ tsp mustard seeds
A big pinch of asafoetida
½ tsp red chilli powder
A few curry leaves
¼ kg field beans, sprouted
½ tsp turmeric powder
Salt to taste

To garnish

Finely chopped coriander and grated coconut

METHOD

Grind together roasted onion, coconut, garlic, cinnamon, cloves, peppercorns and coriander seeds with a little water, to a thick paste.

Heat oil in a thick-bottomed pan; add mustard seeds, asafoetida, chilli powder, curry leaves, and fry for a few seconds.

Add sprouted beans and 1 cup water, and cook till almost done Add the spice paste, turmeric powder and salt. Add a little extra water, if required. Cook until the beans are very soft. Garnish with coriander and coconut and serve.

Serves 4-6

Osaman

spicy thin split pigeon pea soup

INGREDIENTS

- ½ cup split pigeon peas
- 1 tsp ginger-chilli paste
- 4-6 *kokum* rinds
- 3-4 tbsp jaggery
- ½ tsp turmeric powder

For tempering

- 1 tbsp ghee
- ¼ tsp fenugreek seeds
- ¼ tsp mustard seeds
- ¼ tsp cumin seeds
- ¼ tsp asafoetida
- A few curry leaves
- 1 green chilli, slit
- 2-inch piece white radish, thinly sliced

To garnish

- Grated coconut and coriander

To serve

- Kathan Dal (page 122) and steamed rice

METHOD

Pressure-cook the split peas with 8-9 cups of water. When cool, whisk well and add ginger-chilli paste, *kokum*, jaggery, and turmeric powder. Bring to a boil and cook for 10-15 minutes.

For tempering, heat ghee in a small pan; add fenugreek seeds, mustard and cumin seeds. When they splutter, add asafoetida, curry leaves, chilli and radish.

Pour tempering over the *dal* and simmer for 10 minutes. Garnish with grated coconut and coriander. Serve hot with *kathan dal* and rice.

Serves 6

Kadhi

spiced yogurt soup

INGREDIENTS

For kadhi

2 cups sour yogurt

4 cups water

6 tbsp gram flour

2-3 tbsp sugar

1½ tbsp salt

¼ tsp asafoetida

1 tbsp ginger-chilli paste

For tempering

1 tbsp ghee

1 tsp cumin seeds

1 tsp mustard seeds

½ tsp fenugreek seeds

1-2 cinnamon sticks

3-4 cloves

3-4 dried round red chillies

2-inch piece white radish, cut into long strips

A few curry leaves

To garnish

Fresh coriander

To serve

Steamed rice

METHOD

Combine all the ingredients for the *kadhi* and beat well with an egg beater or whisk. For tempering, heat the ghee in a small pan; add the cumin seeds, mustard and fenugreek seeds and fry till they splutter.

Add the remaining ingredients and fry for half a minute. Pour the spices into the *kadhi*, place on heat and bring to a boil. Stir frequently to prevent lumps from forming. Cook till the *kadhi* thickens. Sprinkle with coriander and serve hot with rice.

Serves 6-8

Kadhi (recipe on adjacent page)

Trevati Dal (recipe on adjacent page)

Trevati Dal

trio of curried lentils

INGREDIENTS

¼ cup split Bengal gram
¼ cup split green gram
¼ cup split pigeon peas
2 tbsp oil
2 dried red chillies
2 cloves, crushed
2 bay leaves
A pinch of asafoetida
½-inch ginger, finely chopped
3 garlic cloves, finely chopped
2 green chillies, finely chopped
1 medium onion, finely chopped
1 medium tomato, finely chopped
Salt to taste
A pinch of turmeric powder
1 tbsp lemon juice
3 tbsp coriander leaves

To serve

Steamed rice and *papad*

METHOD

Soak all the varieties of gram and peas for one hour and pressure cook till the pressure is released three to four times (3-4 whistles). Set aside to cool.

Heat oil in a pan; add dried chillies, cloves, bay leaves and asafoetida. Fry until they turn brown. Add chopped ginger, garlic, chillies and fry for 4-5 minutes. Add onion and tomato, salt and turmeric powder and cook until soft.

Beat the cooked *dal* with a whisk and add 2 cups of water. Simmer for a few minutes. Add the lemon juice and coriander and stir well.

Serve hot with rice and *papad*.

Serves 6

Lachko Dal/Kathan Dal

thick split green gram curry

INGREDIENTS

1 cup skinless split green gram
1 inch ginger
$^1/_4$ tsp turmeric powder
1 tbsp ghee
$^1/_4$ tsp asafoetida
Salt to taste

To serve

Steamed rice, Kadhi (page 118) or Osaman (page 117)

METHOD

Pressure-cook the split gram with 4-5 cups of water, ginger, and turmeric powder till the pressure is released 3-4 times (3-4 whistles). Set aside to cool. Drain and reserve water to use in *kadhi* or *osaman.* Heat ghee in a small pan; add asafoetida and when it sizzles, pour over cooked split gram. Whisk the cooked gram till smooth. Return to heat, add salt and cook on a low heat for about 10 minutes till thick. Remove from heat and serve with rice.

Serves 4-6

Ugela Mug

curried sprouted green gram

INGREDIENTS

1 cup whole green gram
2 tbsp oil
$^1/_4$ tsp asafoetida
3 green chillies, slit
2-3 garlic cloves
$^1/_4$ cup finely chopped coriander
2 onions, finely chopped
2 tsp ginger-chilli paste
$^1/_4$ tsp turmeric powder
1 tsp *garam masala*
Salt to taste
2 tomatoes, finely chopped
Juice of $^1/_2$ lemon

METHOD

Soak green gram overnight or for 8 hours. Drain and tie in a piece of muslin and place in a covered bowl to sprout for at least 12 hours. Heat oil in a pan; add asafoetida, chillies, garlic and coriander and fry for 1 minute. Add onions and ginger-chilli paste and cook half a minute longer. Add sprouted gram and turmeric powder, along with 1 cup water, *garam masala* and salt. Cover and cook until tender. Add tomatoes and lemon juice and cook for 5 more minutes. Serve hot.

Serves 4-6

Fajeto
mango-yogurt curry

INGREDIENTS

1 medium ripe mango
2 cups water
1 tbsp gram flour
1 tsp sugar
1 tsp ginger-chilli paste
1 tsp chilli powder
Salt to taste
½ cup yogurt, beaten

For tempering

1 tbsp ghee
3-4 cinnamon sticks
3-4 cloves
5-6 curry leaves
½ tsp cumin seeds
1 green chilli, broken

To garnish

Finely chopped coriander

To serve

Steamed rice

METHOD

Peel and cut the mango. Add ½ cup of water and process in a blender. Pass through a strainer to get a smooth purée. Add the remaining water, gram flour, sugar, ginger-chilli paste, chilli powder and salt and mix well.

For tempering, heat ghee in a thick-bottomed pan; add all the tempering ingredients and then add the mango mixture. Bring to a boil, lower the heat and simmer for 5-10 minutes. Add beaten yogurt and mix well.

Garnish with coriander and serve hot with rice.

Serves 4-6

Khatta Mug

green gram in tangy gravy

INGREDIENTS

⅓ cup whole green gram
Salt to taste
1½ cups sour yogurt
⅓ cup gram flour
1 tsp ginger-chilli paste
1 tsp sugar
¼ tsp turmeric powder

For tempering

1 tbsp ghee
¼ tsp mustard seeds
¼ tsp fenugreek seeds
2-3 dried red chillies
A pinch of asafoetida
7-8 curry leaves

To garnish

Finely chopped coriander

To serve

Steamed rice

METHOD

Pressure-cook green gram with a little salt until tender. Mix yogurt with 5 cups of water and gram flour; whisk the mixture till smooth. Add ginger-chilli paste, sugar, turmeric powder and salt. Mix together cooked gram and yogurt mixture in a pan and bring to a boil stirring occasionally.

For tempering, in a small pan heat ghee, and add mustard seeds, fenugreek seeds and chillies. When they splutter, add asafoetida and curry leaves. Add the spices to the boiling green gram. Cook for 5 more minutes. Garnish with chopped coriander and serve with rice.

Serves 2

Chhuti Mug ni Dal

spiced split green gram

INGREDIENTS

1 cup skinless split green gram

2 tbsp oil

½ tsp mustard seeds

2-3 cinnamon sticks

2-3 cloves

1 inch ginger

1 green chilli

A pinch of asafoetida

4-5 curry leaves

¼ tsp turmeric powder

Salt to taste

1 tsp lemon juice

To garnish

Chopped coriander and grated coconut

To serve

Steamed rice and Kadhi (page 118)

METHOD

Wash and soak split gram for 2 hours. Drain and set aside. Heat the oil in a wide pan; add mustard seeds, cinnamon, cloves, ginger and chilli. When the seeds begin to splutter, add asafoetida and curry leaves.

Add the drained *dal*, turmeric powder and salt. Add 1 cup water, cover and cook on a low heat till *dal* is soft. Do not stir too much or else *dal* grains will not remain separate. Stir in the lemon juice. Garnish with coriander and coconut. Serve with rice and *kadhi*.

Serves 4

Tameta ane Shaak ni Kadhi

tomato and vegetable curry

INGREDIENTS

1 cup split pigeon peas

8-10 medium tomatoes, cut into thick slices

3 cups water

Salt to taste

200 gm small ladies' fingers, cut into 2-inch pieces and boiled

200 gm drumsticks, cut into 2-inch pieces and boiled

200 gm French beans, cut into 2-inch pieces and boiled

200 gm carrots, cut into 2-inch pieces and boiled

For tempering

3 tbsp oil

1 tsp cumin seeds

½ tsp fenugreek seeds

3-4 green chillies, slit

A few curry leaves

A pinch of asafoetida

3 tbsp gram flour

1 tsp red chilli powder

½ tsp turmeric powder

To garnish

Finely chopped coriander leaves

To serve

Steamed Basmati rice and *papad*

METHOD

Wash and soak the split peas for 1 hour before cooking. Place soaked split peas, tomatoes and 3 cups of water in a pressure cooker and cook till the pressure is released once (1 whistle). Reduce heat and cook, till pressure is released twice (2 whistles). Allow the cooker to cool. Whisk the *dal* and add hot water if necessary, till you get a smooth, soupy consistency.

For tempering, heat the oil in a pan on medium heat. Add the cumin and fenugreek seeds, chillies, curry leaves and asafoetida. Once the seeds stop spluttering, add gram flour and continue cooking till the gram flour is pale brown and cooked. Add chilli powder and turmeric powder and turn off the heat. Add the spices to the *dal*. Season with salt. Add the boiled vegetables and cook for 3-4 minutes. Garnish with coriander leaves and serve piping hot with Basmati rice and *papad*.

Serves 6

Rotli & Bhakri Vaghere

Indian Breads

Rotli

wholewheat flatbread

INGREDIENTS

1 cup wholewheat flour
+ for dusting

1 tsp oil

½ tsp salt

Ghee (optional) as required

METHOD

Mix the flour, oil and salt with enough warm water to make a dough. Knead the dough well and set aside for half an hour. Knead again.

Divide into 6 portions and roll out each one into a 6-inch disc, dusting with a little flour while rolling out the *rotlis*.

Heat a *tawa* and cook each *rotli* lightly on both sides. Brush with a little ghee if desired and keep warm.

Makes 6 *rotlis*

Bhaat na Thepla
spiced rice flatbread

INGREDIENTS

¾ cup cooked rice
½ cup sour yogurt
½ cup gram flour
½ cup wholewheat flour
+ for dusting
¼ cup rice flour
1 tsp chilli powder
½ tsp turmeric powder
2 tbsp finely chopped coriander
Salt to taste
Oil for shallow-frying

To serve

Vegetable dish, pickle and yogurt

METHOD

Soak rice in yogurt for half an hour, or overnight in a refrigerator. Add the remaining ingredients, and a little water to the soaked rice and knead to make a moderately soft dough. Cover and set aside for 15 minutes.

Divide the dough into 10-12 balls. Roll out each ball to a 5-inch disc, dusting with a little wholewheat flour. Cook each *thepla* on both sides on a hot *tawa*, drizzling with a little oil. Serve hot with a vegetable dish, pickle and yogurt.

Makes 10-12 *theplas*

Khari Puri
savoury puffed breads

INGREDIENTS

1 cup wholewheat flour
1 tbsp gram flour
½ tsp chilli powder
¼ tsp turmeric powder
A pinch of asafoetida
½ tsp salt
1 tbsp oil + for deep-frying

To serve

Vegetable dish

METHOD

Mix together all the flours, powdered spices, salt, 1 tablespoon oil and enough water and knead to make a stiff dough. Cover and set aside for half an hour.

Knead well and shape into 12-15 balls. Roll them out into small discs. Heat oil in *kadai* and deep-fry the *puri* in batches, 2-3 at a time. Serve hot with a vegetable dish.

Makes 12-15 *puris*

Gujarati Puran Poli

sweet stuffed flatbread

INGREDIENTS

For puran

1 cup split pigeon peas

1½ cups sugar

¼ tsp powdered cardamom

For poli

1 cup wholewheat flour + for dusting

1 tbsp ghee + for shallow-frying

METHOD

For puran

Cook split peas in enough water until soft. Drain extra water when cooked. In a thick-bottomed pan, add cooked *dal* and sugar and cook, stirring continuously, until the mixture is thick. Remove from heat and cool.

Add cardamom to the cooled *puran* mixture; make walnut-sized balls and set aside.

For poli

Mix together flour, ghee and enough water and knead to make a soft dough. Set aside for 10-15 minutes. Divide the dough in 12-14 parts. Roll out each part into a 3-inch disc.

Place a portion of *puran* in the centre and bring the edges together to enclose the filling. Press down gently and roll out into a 4-5 inch disc. Heat a *tawa* and cook *puran poli* on both sides with a little ghee.

Makes 12-14 *puran polis*

Bajri-Methi na Thepla

millet and fenugreek flatbread

INGREDIENTS

1 cup wholewheat flour
1 cup millet flour
¼ tsp turmeric powder
1 tsp chilli powder
1 tsp coriander-cumin powder
Salt to taste
1 cup fresh fenugreek leaves
2 tbsp oil + for shallow-frying
1 tsp ginger-chilli paste
2 tsp jaggery
Sour yogurt to bind the dough

To serve

Vegetable dish,
Chhundo (page 80) or *raita*

METHOD

Mix together both flours, powdered spices, salt, fenugreek leaves, 2 tablespoons oil, ginger-chilli paste, jaggery and yogurt, and knead to make a moderately soft dough. Do not add water. Divide the dough into 12-14 balls.

Roll out each ball into a 4-5-inch thin disc. Cook the *thepla* on a preheated greased *tawa* over a medium heat. Drizzle oil with a small teaspoon around the edge of the *thepla*. Cook on both sides. Remove from heat when *thepla* is completely cooked. Serve hot with a vegetable dish, *chhundo* or *raita* or as a teatime snack.

Makes 12-14 *theplas*

Note: You can replace fenugreek leaves with grated bottle gourd.

Saat Dhaan-Methi Rotli

seven grain-fenugreek flatbread

INGREDIENTS

- 1/4 cup millet flour
- 1/4 cup sorghum flour
- 1/4 cup maize flour
- 1/4 cup soy flour
- 1/4 cup finger millet flour
- 1/4 cup wholewheat flour
- 2 tbsp gram flour
- 1 cup finely chopped fenugreek leaves
- Salt to taste

METHOD

Mix all the flours together and transfer to an airtight jar. Store in a refrigerator. For 1 cup flour mixture, use 1 cup fenugreek leaves. Add salt and water and knead to make a soft dough. Set aside for half an hour.

Roll out into 6-inch thin discs and dry-roast on a *tawa* until they puff up. Serve at once.

Makes 12-14 *rotlis*

Dudhi Thepla

spicy bottle gourd flatbread

INGREDIENTS

1 cup wholewheat flour
1 cup millet flour
¼ tsp turmeric powder
1 tsp chilli powder
1 tsp coriander-cumin powder
Salt to taste
1 cup grated bottle gourd
2 tbsp oil
A pinch of soda bicarbonate
Sour yogurt to bind the dough
1 tsp ginger-chilli paste
Oil for shallow-frying

To serve

Raita

METHOD

Mix together both the flours, powdered spices, salt, bottle gourd, 2 tablespoons oil and soda bicarbonate. Add enough yogurt and ginger-chilli paste, and knead to make a moderately soft dough. Do not add water. Divide the dough into 12-14 balls. Roll out each one into a thin disc.

Cook the *thepla* on a *tawa* over medium heat, using a little oil. Pour oil with a small teaspoon around the edge of the *thepla*. Turn over and repeat the process. Remove from heat when the *thepla* is completely cooked. Serve hot with *raita* or as a teatime snack.

Makes 12-14

Note: You can replace bottle gourd with fenugreek leaves.

Bhakri
crisp wholewheat flatbread

INGREDIENTS

2 cups wholewheat flour
6 tbsp ghee
Salt to taste

METHOD

Place the flour in a rimmed platter (*thali*); make a well in the centre and add ghee and salt. Add enough water and knead to make a stiff dough. Set aside, covered, for half an hour. Knead the dough again to make it smooth and elastic and divide it into 10-12 equal balls.

Heat a *tawa*. Roll out the balls into 3-inch discs, and dry-roast on the *tawa*, on low heat. Flip and roast the other side as well. Press the *bhakri* down lightly on the *tawa* in a circular movement with the help of a thick wad of cloth or a wooden press. Turn over and press again to ensure that the *bhakri* is crisp and brown. Serve hot.

Serves 6

Chopda

layered flatbread

INGREDIENTS

- 2 cups wholewheat flour + for dusting
- 3 tbsp oil
- 1 tsp cumin seeds
- Salt to taste
- Oil or ghee, as required

To serve

- Vegetable dish

METHOD

Mix together flour, oil, cumin seeds, a little salt and water and knead to make a soft dough. Set aside, covered, for 30 minutes. Divide the dough into 12-14 balls. Flatten each ball, dust the work surface with a little flour and roll out into a 4-inch disc. Brush oil or ghee on the surface and fold to a quarter to make a triangle. Roll out the triangle, keeping the shape intact.

Cook on a preheated *tawa* on a medium heat, drizzling oil around the edges. Turn over and repeat the process to cook the other side. Cook, pressing down lightly with a flat spoon or spatula, until brown and slightly crisp. Serve hot with a vegetable dish.

Makes 12-14 *chopda*

Chopda (recipe on adjacent page)

Bhakri (recipe on page 135)

Dudhi Thepla (recipe on page 134)

Bhaat & Pulav Vaghere

Rice

Hariyali Pulav

green chutney and vegetable pilaf

INGREDIENTS

For green chutney

2 cups coriander leaves
4-5 spinach leaves
1-inch ginger
4-5 green chillies
2-3 garlic cloves
1 tsp lemon juice
Salt to taste

For rice

4 tbsp ghee
2-3 cinnamon sticks
2-3 cloves
2-3 peppercorns
2-3 cardamoms
2 bay leaves
2 pieces onions, thinly sliced
2 green chillies
200 gm cauliflower or broccoli
200 gm sliced potatoes
½ cup shelled green peas
1 tsp *garam masala*
Salt to taste
1 cup Basmati rice, washed, soaked and cooked

To garnish

Finely chopped coriander and spring onion

To serve

Coconut Sauce (page 61)

METHOD

For chutney

Grind together all the ingredients to make a smooth paste.

For rice

Heat 1 tbsp ghee in a frying pan and fry cinnamon, cloves, peppercorns, cardamoms and bay leaves for half a minute. Add sliced onions and chillies and cook until the onions turn transparent. Set aside.

In a wide pan, heat remaining ghee and fry the vegetables for 4-5 minutes. Add the chutney and cook for 1 minute. Add fried onion mixture, *garam masala*, salt and rice. Mix well. Transfer rice to a serving dish, garnish with coriander and spring onions and serve hot with coconut sauce.

Serves 4

Makai-Masala Bhaat

spiced rice with corn

INGREDIENTS

4-5 tbsp ghee

¼ tsp asafoetida

1 tsp mustard seeds

4-5 green chillies

2-3 cinnamon sticks

2-3 cloves

½ tsp turmeric powder

1 medium onion, chopped long

½ cup corn kernels, boiled

10-12 pieces ivy gourds, cut into 4 pieces lengthways

1½ cups rice, washed, and soaked in water for 10 minutes and drained

2 tsp *kala masala*

2 tsp *garam masala*

1 tsp chilli powder

Salt to taste

2 tbsp cashew nuts, chopped

A few curry leaves

2 tbsp chopped fresh coconut

1 tsp lemon juice

1 tsp ginger juice

To garnish

¼ cup freshly chopped coriander

To serve

Spiced Yogurt (page 149)

METHOD

Heat the ghee in a thick-bottomed pan; add asafoetida and mustard seeds. When they splutter, add green chillies, cinnamon, cloves and turmeric powder. Add onion, corn and ivy gourds. Cook for 2-3 minutes and add the rice and all the spice powders. Stir and add 3 cups water. Cover and cook on low heat for 15 minutes, stirring occasionally.

Add salt, cashew nuts, curry leaves, coconut, lemon and ginger juice and cook till rice is soft. Remove from heat and garnish with coriander and serve with spiced yogurt.

Serves 4-6

Note: You can use any vegetables you like, such as French beans, brinjal etc.

Trirangi Bhaat

tri-coloured rice with tempered yogurt

INGREDIENTS

For rice

2 cups rice, washed and soaked
½ cup tomato purée
Salt to taste
1 tsp red chilli powder
4 tbsp ghee or butter
½ tsp turmeric powder
½ cup corn kernels, boiled
Juice of 1 lemon
1 medium onion, finely chopped
2 tbsp cashew nuts, chopped

To garnish

Fried onions and tomato slices

For tempered yogurt

2 cups thick yogurt
1 tbsp oil
1 tsp mustard seeds
½ tsp asafoetida
2-3 dried round red chillies
A few curry leaves
1 tsp powdered sugar
Salt to taste
1 tbsp coriander leaves, finely chopped

METHOD

For rice

Cook the rice in 4 cups of water making sure the grains remain separate. Divide the rice into 3 parts.

For the red layer, mix together the tomato purée, salt and chilli powder. Add this to one part of the rice and set aside.

For the yellow layer, heat 1 tablespoon ghee. Add turmeric and corn. Fry for 1 minute, then add the second part of rice, lemon juice and salt, mix well and set aside.

For the white layer, heat 1 tablespoon ghee and sauté the onions. When soft, add the cashew nuts and fry for 1 minute. Add the third part of rice and salt, mix and set aside.

To assemble

Take an 8-inch round baking dish or if you wish to invert the mould, use an aluminium mould. Grease the dish with ghee. Spread the red layer evenly at the bottom of the dish, pressing down with your palm. Brush a little ghee on top. Spread the yellow and white rice one on top of the other in the same way. Cover the dish and bake in a hot oven at 180°C/350°F/Gas Mark 4 for 10-12 minutes. Remove from the oven, unmould on a serving dish. Garnish with fried onions and tomatoes and serve hot with tempered yogurt.

For tempered yogurt

Beat the yogurt and set aside. Heat the oil in a small pan and add mustard seeds. When they start spluttering, add asafoetida, dried chillies and curry leaves.

Fry for half a minute, take it off the heat and add this to the yogurt. Add sugar, salt and chopped coriander. Chill until ready to serve.

~ Serves 4-6

Palak ne Tameta na Bhaat

spinach and tomato layered rice

INGREDIENTS

- 1 tbsp ghee
- 2-3 cinnamon sticks
- 2-3 cloves
- 2-3 cardamoms
- 2 cups Basmati rice, washed and soaked for ½ hour
- 5 cups water

For spinach layer

- 1 tbsp ghee
- 1 large onion, chopped
- 2 tbsp ginger
- 2 tbsp finely chopped green chillies
- 2 cups spinach leaves, boiled and mashed
- 1 tsp *garam masala*
- Salt to taste
- 200 gm cottage cheese, cubed

For tomato layer

- 6 medium tomatoes, blanched and chopped
- ½ cup fresh cream
- Salt to taste
- Pepper powder to taste
- Sugar to taste
- Chilli powder to taste

To garnish

- Sliced and fried onions, fried almonds or cashew nuts

To serve

- Yogurt or Kadhi (page 118)

METHOD

Heat ghee in a thick-bottomed pan; add cinnamon, cloves and cardamoms. Fry until fragrant. Add soaked and drained rice and cook until the rice is coated with ghee. Add water and cook the rice until almost done and take off heat. Spread rice in a large plate. Leave to cool.

For spinach layer

Heat ghee in a pan and fry onion, ginger and chillies for 1 minute. Add the spinach, *garam masala* and salt. Cook for 1 more minute and add cottage cheese. Remove from heat. Add half the rice to this mixture and toss gently to mix.

For tomato layer

Mix the tomatoes, cream, salt, pepper powder, sugar and chilli powder in a bowl. Add remaining rice to this mixture.

In an 8x9-inch heatproof mould, spread the spinach rice. Spread the tomato rice over the spinach rice layer. Cover the mould and bake at 200°C/400°F/Gas Mark 6 for 15-20 minutes. Unmould the rice on a serving plate and garnish with fried onions and nuts. Serve hot with yogurt or *kadhi*.

Serves 8

Vagharela Bhaat

quick spiced rice

INGREDIENTS

2-3 tbsp ghee

1 tsp mustard seeds

1 tsp cumin seeds

A pinch of asafoetida

2-3 green chillies, cut into ½-inch pieces

5-6 curry leaves

2 medium onions, finely chopped

1-2 tbsp *biryani masala*

½ tsp turmeric powder

3 cups cooked rice

½ tsp sugar

Lemon juice to taste

Salt to taste

To garnish

Finely chopped coriander

To serve

Plain yogurt

METHOD

Heat ghee in a wide pan; add mustard and cumin seeds. When they splutter, add asafoetida, chillies, curry leaves and onions. Cook until onions soften.

Add *biryani masala* and turmeric powder. Add cooked rice, sugar, lemon juice and salt. Toss gently to mix. Garnish with coriander and serve with plain yogurt.

Tip: Add 1 finely chopped tomato after onions soften, or half a cup of boiled peas as a variation.

Serves 4-6

Ek Top na Dal-Bhaat

one-pot spicy rice and lentils

INGREDIENTS

2 cups Basmati rice
¼ cup ghee
4-5 cloves
1-2 cinnamon sticks
3-4 cardamoms
1½ cups split pigeon peas
½ cup skinless split green gram
200 gm ivy gourd
¼ tsp turmeric powder
¼ tsp asafoetida
Salt to taste
2 cups hot water
1½ cups fresh coriander, finely chopped
¾ cup grated fresh coconut
1 tbsp sugar
A pinch of asafoetida
½ tsp turmeric powder
½ tsp red chilli powder
1 tbsp ginger-chilli paste
1 tsp coriander-cumin powder
Juice of 1 lemon
¼ cup gram flour, roasted
6-8 small potatoes, peeled
10 small onions
6-8 small brinjals, stemmed

To serve

Kadhi (page 118)

METHOD

Soak rice for half an hour. Heat ghee in a thick-bottomed pan; add the cloves, cinnamon and cardamom and fry for a minute. Add split peas, split gram, ivy gourd, turmeric powder, asafoetida and enough salt to season. Mix well and add the hot water. Cover and cook on a low heat till the peas, gram, and ivy gourd are half-cooked.

Mix together coriander, coconut, salt, sugar, a pinch of asafoetida, turmeric powder, chilli powder, ginger-chilli paste, coriander-cumin powder, lemon juice and gram flour in a large plate. Slit the potatoes, onions, and brinjals vertically and soak them in water. Stuff the vegetables with the prepared spice mixture. Mix the remaining mixture with the vegetables so that they are well coated with the spices. Arrange them over the partially cooked gram. Add warm water, as required to cook vegetables. Cover and cook till the vegetables are half cooked.

Spread the rice over the vegetables. Add salt and a little ghee and enough warm water to cook the rice. Cook, covered till all the water has evaporated and the rice is tender. Make sure the peas and gram do not stick to the bottom. To serve, unmould the dish by inverting the pan over a large plate. Serve hot with *kadhi*.

Serves 6-8

Ek Top na Dal-Bhaat
(recipe on adjacent page)

Vagharela Bhaat (recipe on page 145)

Fada ni Khichdi
(recipe on adjacent page)

Kuttu-dara na Dhokla/Khichdi
(recipe on page 154)

Fada ni Khichdi

cracked wheat and gram khichdi

INGREDIENTS

- 1 cup cracked wheat
- ½ cup split green gram
- 1 cup mixed vegetables, finely chopped
- 1-inch ginger
- 1½ cups tomatoes, boiled and strained
- Salt to taste

For tempering

- 3 tbsp ghee
- 1 cinnamon stick
- 3-4 cloves
- ¼ tsp turmeric powder
- ¼ tsp asafoetida
- ½ tsp chilli powder
- 1 tsp *garam masala*
- 1 tbsp ginger-chilli paste

To serve

- Spiced Yogurt

METHOD

Wash and soak cracked wheat and split gram separately for half an hour. Mix this with chopped vegetables, ginger and 2 cups of hot water and cook in a pressure cooker till the pressure is released thrice (3 whistles). Leave to cool. After about 20 minutes, uncover the cooker and churn the mixture with a wooden churner to make the mixture smooth. If the mixture is too dry, add a little hot water. Add tomato purée and salt to taste and mix well.

Transfer the mixture to a heavy-bottomed pan and cook on low heat. In a small pan, heat ghee, add all the tempering ingredients, one after the other, and let them sizzle. Add to the wheat mixture, stirring vigorously to mix. Serve hot with spiced yogurt.

Serves 4-6

SPICED YOGURT

To make spiced yogurt, add salt, sugar, cumin powder, chilli powder and chopped coriander to yogurt, mix well and serve.

Baked Khichdi

baked spiced rice with sprouts

INGREDIENTS

1 cup long grain rice, washed and soaked

Salt to taste

¼ cup whole green gram, soaked overnight

¼ cup black-eyed beans, soaked overnight

2-3 tbsp ghee

1 tsp cumin seeds

1-2 tbsp ginger-garlic-chilli paste

2 medium onions, finely chopped

1 tsp chilli powder

1 tsp *garam masala*

A pinch of turmeric powder

A pinch of asafoetida

2 medium tomatoes, finely chopped

½ cup tomato juice

½ cup cottage cheese

½ cup yogurt

To garnish

Soft fried onions, freshly chopped coriander

METHOD

Cook rice in 2 cups of boiling water with a little salt. Make sure the grains are separate. Set aside. Boil the green gram and beans in water, until soft. Drain and set aside.

Heat ghee in a wide-bottomed pan and add cumin seeds followed by ginger-garlic-chilli paste. Fry for 1 minute. Add onions and cook until soft. Add all the spices with tomatoes and cook until fragrant. Add the boiled gram and beans, rice, tomato juice and salt. Do not over cook the *khichdi*.

Transfer the *khichdi* to a greased baking dish. Mix cottage cheese, yogurt and a little salt in a blender till smooth. Spread a thin layer of the mixture over the *khichdi*. Sprinkle soft fried onions on top and bake in a hot oven at 325°F/170°C/Gas Mark 3 for 10-12 minutes. Garnish with chopped coriander and serve at once.

Serves 4

Masala Khichdi

rice and legumes cooked with spices

INGREDIENTS

For khichdi

- 3/4 cup rice
- 1/4 cup split pigeon peas OR split green gram
- 1 1/2 tomatoes, boiled, puréed and strained
- 1 cup finely chopped mixed boiled vegetables
- 1 tbsp coriander leaves

For tempering

- 1 tbsp ghee or butter
- 1/4 tsp turmeric powder
- 1/2 tsp coriander-cumin powder
- 1/2 tsp chilli powder
- 1/2 tsp *garam masala*
- 1/2 tsp green chilli-ginger paste

To serve

- Yogurt

METHOD

Soak the rice for 15-20 minutes and drain. Soak the split gram for 30 minutes and drain. Boil 2 cups of water in a large thick-bottomed pan on high heat, and add rice and gram. Lower the heat and cook for 20 minutes until the rice and gram are tender.

Melt the ghee in a pan, on medium heat. Add all the ingredients and fry for a few seconds. Add strained tomatoes and vegetables. Add the mixture and coriander to rice and gram. Cook over low heat for 10 minutes more with the lid on. Serve hot with yogurt.

Serves 4-6

Saat Dhaan ni Khichdi

seven grain pilaf

INGREDIENTS

- 1 tbsp whole green gram
- 1 tbsp whole red lentil
- 1 tbsp moth beans (*muth*)
- 1 tbsp black-eyed peas
- 1 tbsp Bengal gram
- 2 tbsp oil
- 3 medium onions, chopped
- 2 tbsp coriander-cumin powder
- 1 tbsp red chilli powder
- 1 tbsp *garam masala*
- ½ tsp turmeric powder
- 1½ cups cracked millet, washed and soaked
- 1 tbsp brown rice
- Salt to taste

To be ground into a paste

- 4 green chillies
- 1-inch ginger
- 8-10 garlic cloves

To garnish

- 2 tbsp chopped coriander

To serve

- Beaten yogurt

METHOD

Soak the legumes overnight. Heat oil in a pressure cooker or a large thick-bottomed pan, and sauté onions until transparent. Add the ground paste along with spice powders and mix well. Add millet, rice and legumes with 5 cups of water and salt. Mix well and cook until the pressure is released 3-4 times (3-4 whistles).

Alternatively, cook in the pan for 35-40 minutes. Remove from heat and stir the mixture with a ladle. Add a little water if the mixture is dry. Adjust salt and transfer to a serving bowl. Garnish with coriander and serve hot with beaten yogurt.

Serves 8

Farali Vangi

Fasting Foods

Kuttu-dara na Dhokla/Khichdi

steamed buckwheat cakes or porridge

INGREDIENTS

For dhokla

1 cup cracked buckwheat (*kuttu-dara*), washed and soaked in a little water

½ cup sour yogurt

1 tbsp ginger-chilli paste

1 tbsp chopped coriander

2 tbsp ghee

Salt to taste

Ghee for greasing

To serve

Green Chutney (page 48)

For khichdi

1 tbsp ghee

½ tsp cumin seeds

1-2 green chillies, chopped

A few curry leaves

1 medium potato, boiled and cut into small cubes

1 recipe Dhokla

2-3 tbsp roasted and coarsely ground peanuts

1 tbsp sugar

1 tbsp lemon juice

Salt to taste

To garnish

Finely chopped coriander and grated coconut

To serve

Yogurt

METHOD

For dhokla

Rinse the soaked buckwheat. Soak in yogurt in a bowl for 10 minutes. Add ginger-chilli paste, coriander, ghee and salt. Mix well.

Place *dhokla* steamer on heat with water and place a steel ring in the centre. Grease a 10-inch round stainless steel plate with rim (*thali*) with ghee and pour the prepared mixture onto it. Place the plate on the ring, in boiling water. Cover tightly with the lid. Steam for 10-12 minutes. Remove from heat and set aside to cool slightly. Cut into squares and serve hot with green chutney.

For khichdi

Heat ghee in a thick-bottomed pan; add cumin seeds, green chillies and curry leaves. Cook for 2-3 minutes; add potato and cook for another 2-3 minutes. Crumble cooled *dhokla* and add to the potato. Mix well. Add peanuts, sugar, lemon juice and salt. Garnish with coriander and grated coconut. Serve hot with yogurt.

Serves 4-6

Rajgara na Thepla

amaranth grain flatbread

INGREDIENTS

1 cup *rajgara* flour

1 small potato, boiled, peeled and mashed

1 tsp ginger-chilli paste

1 tbsp finely chopped coriander

1 tbsp yogurt

Salt to taste

Ghee for roasting

METHOD

Mix together flour, mashed potato, ginger-chilli paste, coriander, yogurt and salt. Add enough water to bind and knead to a soft dough. Divide the dough into 6 portions.

This dough is very difficult to roll, so cut a square piece of plastic and place on a work surface. Place a piece of dough and place another piece of plastic over it, and roll out the dough into a 4-inch disc. Dust with some *rajgara* flour to prevent the dough from sticking. Heat a thick-bottomed *tawa*, place the *thepla* on the *tawa*, drizzle 1 teaspoon ghee around it. Cook on both sides and serve hot with vegetable or chutney.

Makes 6 *theplas*

Farali Misal

crisp snack

INGREDIENTS

- 100 gm purple yam
- 100 gm sweet potato
- 100 gm elephant's foot yam
- 100 gm potato
- 100 gm bottle gourd
- 2½ cups sour yogurt
- 3 cups water
- 2-3 tbsp arrowroot flour
- Salt to taste
- 1 tbsp ghee
- 1 tbsp cumin seeds
- 1-2 green chillies, cut into pieces
- 6-8 curry leaves
- 1½ tbsp ginger-chilli paste
- 1½ tbsp sugar
- ½ cup raw peanuts, boiled

To garnish

Finely chopped coriander, grated coconut, fine potato straws and lemon wedges

METHOD

Cut the purple yam, sweet potato, yam, potato and bottle gourd into cubes and boil.

Mix together yogurt, water, arrowroot and little salt in a bowl and whisk until the arrowroot has dissolved. Set aside. In a medium pan, heat ghee; add cumin seeds and when they splutter, add chillies and curry leaves. Cook for 1 minute and add yogurt mixture.

Add all the remaining ingredients and allow *misal* to cook on a low heat, until the gravy thickens slightly.

To serve

Misal is served in individual bowls. Spoon ½ cup of hot *misal* into a bowl; garnish with coriander, coconut and potato straws. Serve with lemon wedges.

Serves 8

Turia, Narial na Dudh ma

ridge gourd in coconut milk

INGREDIENTS

- 1 tbsp ghee
- 1 tsp cumin seeds
- 1 green chilli
- A few curry leaves
- ½ kg ridge gourd, peeled and cut into 1-inch pieces
- 2 cups fresh coconut milk
- 1 tbsp arrowroot flour
- 1 tbsp ginger-chilli paste
- Sugar to taste
- Salt to taste

To serve

- Rajgara Na Thepla (page 155)

METHOD

Heat ghee in a thick-bottomed pan; add cumin seeds, chilli and curry leaves and fry for a few seconds. Add ridge gourd and mix well. Cover and cook on medium heat. You can pour some water on the lid to prevent the vegetable from sticking. Stir occasionally.

When the vegetable is completely cooked, add coconut milk mixed with arrowroot flour. Add ginger-chilli paste, sugar and salt. Serve hot with *rajgara na thepla*.

Serves 4

Vagharela Bhavnagari Marcha

spiced chillies

INGREDIENTS

2 tbsp oil

½ tsp sesame seeds

½ tsp cumin seeds

2 tbsp water chestnut flour

1 cup sliced Bhavnagari chillies

½ tbsp lemon juice

Rock salt to taste

METHOD

Heat the oil in a non-stick *kadai* and add the sesame seeds and cumin seeds.

When the seeds splutter, add the water chestnut flour and cook on a low heat for 2-3 minutes, stirring continuously, till the flour is cooked.

Add the chillies, lemon juice and rock salt and cook on a low heat for 5 minutes, stirring once in between.

Serve immediately.

Makes ½ cup

Farali Kand No Handvo

savoury yam pie

INGREDIENTS

- 1 kg purple yam, boiled and mashed
- 2 medium potatoes, boiled and mashed
- 2-3 tbsp thick yogurt
- Salt to taste
- Juice of 1 lemon
- 4 tbsp freshly grated coconut
- 4 tbsp coriander, finely chopped
- 2 tbsp green chilli-ginger paste
- ½ cup roasted and crushed peanuts
- Sugar to taste
- 2 tbsp ghee for greasing
- A greased 8-inch square or 6x9-inch rectangular baking dish

For tempering

- 2 tbsp ghee
- 1 tsp cumin seeds
- 4-5 green chillies, chopped
- A few curry leaves

To garnish

- Freshly grated coconut and freshly chopped coriander

To serve

- Green Chutney (page 48) or Coconut Sauce (page 61)

METHOD

Mix together mashed yam, potatoes and yogurt, and season with salt, and juice of half a lemon, and set aside. In a small bowl, mix together coconut, coriander, ginger-chilli paste, peanuts, sugar, salt and remaining lemon juice.

Grease the baking dish; spread half the yam and potato mixture, layer coconut-coriander mixture and spread evenly. Finally spread a layer of the remaining yam mixture and smooth the top with your palms.

For tempering

Heat ghee in a small pan, add cumin seeds and when they splutter add chillies and curry leaves. Remove from heat and add 1 tablespoon water.

Drizzle the tempering evenly over the yam mixture and bake in a hot oven at 180°C/350°F/Gas Mark 4, for 15-20 minutes. Allow it to rest for 4-5 minutes and then cut into 1-inch squares and serve hot with green chutney or coconut sauce.

Serves 6-8

Farali Lili Chutney

coriander and peanut chutney

INGREDIENTS

- 2 cups coriander leaves, finely chopped
- ½ cup grated coconut
- ¼ cup roasted peanuts
- 3-4 green chillies
- 1 inch ginger
- 1 tbsp sugar
- ½ tsp cumin seeds
- Juice of 1 lemon
- Salt to taste

METHOD

Grind together all the ingredients to make a coarse paste. Serve with savory snacks.

Makes 1 cup

Mithai & Ice Cream

Desserts

Sitafal Ice Cream

custard apple ice cream

INGREDIENTS

- 1½ litres milk
- ¾-1 cup sugar
- 2 tbsp custard powder
- 1 cup custard apple pulp
- 1 tsp vanilla essence
- 200 gm whipping cream, whipped

METHOD

Boil the milk in a thick-bottomed pan for 15 minutes. Add sugar and cook for 10 more minutes. Blend custard powder in a little cold milk and add to the boiling milk. Stir and cook for another 2-3 minutes. Remove from heat and set aside to cool. Mix custard apple pulp, vanilla and whipped cream to the cooled milk. Make ice cream in the ice cream maker or transfer to an aluminium container and freeze until set.

Serves 8-10

Lychee Ice Cream

INGREDIENTS

- 2 cups lychee pulp (of approx. 30 lychees)
- ½ tsp lemon juice
- 1 cup sugar
- 1 tbsp unflavoured gelatine
- ½ cup chopped lychees
- 200 gm fresh cream
- 2 cups milk, boiled for 20 minutes and cooled

METHOD

Mix together lychee pulp, lemon juice and sugar. Mix gelatine in a little water and add to the lychee pulp. Heat the mixture on low heat and cook until sugar melts and the gelatine is dissolved. Remove from heat and set aside to cool.

Add chopped lychees, cream and milk. Mix well till all the ingredients are properly combined. Pour into a metal container, cover and freeze, or churn it in an ice cream maker till set.

Serves 6

Sutarfeni

soft vermicelli triangles with cottage cheese and fresh fruit

INGREDIENTS

1 cup cottage cheese, grated

½ cup icing sugar, sieved

1 tsp cornflour

½ cup fruit of your choice, freshly chopped (pineapple, orange, mango) and chopped mixed dried fruit

250 gm x 2 discs white OR saffron-flavoured *sutarfeni*

¼ cup sugar syrup

To garnish

A few rose petals and slices of fruit

METHOD

In a medium bowl, mix together the cottage cheese, icing sugar and cornflour. Add finely chopped fruit. Place 1 *sutarfeni* disc on a lightly greased baking tray and heat slightly, in a moderate oven, just until a little crisp. Remove from the oven and cool slightly.

Place *sutarfeni* on a serving dish and evenly spread the cottage cheese mixture over it. Make the other *sutarfeni* slightly crisp in the oven and place it over the cottage cheese mixture. Pour sugar syrup over the *sutarfeni*, making sure it does not trickle out of the sides. Decorate with rose petals and fruit slices. Cut it into triangles and serve at room temperature or cold.

Serves 6-8

Navratna Basundi

thickened milk with nine fresh and dried fruit

INGREDIENTS

1½ litres milk

A few saffron strands

8 tbsp sugar

½ tsp cardamom powder

½ cup chopped dried fruit and nuts (almonds, cashew nuts, pistachios, glacé cherries and dates)

¾ cup chopped fresh fruit (apples, oranges and grapes)

METHOD

Boil the milk on a low heat till reduced to half. Keep pushing the cream that forms on top to the side of the pan.

Mix saffron in a little milk and add it to hot milk, along with sugar, cardamom powder and dried fruit. Cook for 2-3 minutes. Remove from heat and cool to room temperature. Add fresh fruit and mix well. Transfer to a serving dish and chill before serving.

Serves 6

Navratna Basundi
(recipe on adjacent page)

Sutarfeni (recipe on page 163)

Top: Mewavati (recipe on page 168)
Centre: Badam Katli (recipe on page 169)
Bottom: Kaju Puri nu Sandwich (recipe on page 167)

Kaju Puri nu Sandwich

cashew puri sandwiches

INGREDIENTS

- 16 coin-sized cashew *puris*
- 1/4 cup powdered pistachios
- 1/4 cup powdered almonds
- 1/2 tsp powdered cardamom
- 2 tbsp thick cream
- 2-3 tbsp thick sugar syrup

For saffron cream

- 1/4 cup butter
- 1/2 cup icing sugar
- A few stands of saffron soaked in little milk

METHOD

Warm the cashew *puris* slightly in the oven. In a small bowl, mix together powdered nuts, cardamom, cream and sugar syrup.

Place 1 tablespoon nut mixture on a *puri* and place another *puri* on top to create a sandwich. Set aside. In a small bowl, beat butter and icing sugar until light. Add soaked saffron and beat again. Fill this cream in an icing syringe and pipe small stars on each sandwich. Serve at room temperature.

Makes 8 sandwiches

Mewavati

dried fruit crescents

INGREDIENTS

For dough

- $2\frac{1}{2}$ tbsp hot ghee
- 1 cup plain flour
- $\frac{1}{4}$ cup semolina
- Water to bind the dough
- Ghee for deep-frying

For filling

- $\frac{1}{2}$ cup *mawa/khoya*
- $\frac{1}{2}$ cup powdered sugar
- 3 tbsp chopped almond and pistachios
- 2 tbsp raisins
- $\frac{1}{4}$ tsp powdered cardamom
- A pinch of nutmeg

METHOD

For filling

Place all the ingredients for the filling in a bowl and mix well. Set aside.

For dough

Mix ghee in the flour and semolina, and make a semi-soft dough with water. Set aside for 30 minutes. Divide the dough in 8-10 balls, cover and set aside. Roll each one into 3-inch circles.

Place 1 tablespoon filling in the centre and moisten the edges with water. Fold over the dough to form a half moon shape. Lightly press the edges to seal. You may use a mould to make the crescents as well. Crimp the edges. Repeat with the remaining dough.

Heat ghee in a wide pan and fry *mewavati* on low heat, 3-4 at a time until golden. Drain and set aside. Leave to cool completely and store in an airtight container. Use as required.

Makes 8-10 *mewavati*

Note: You can also replace *mawa* with desiccated coconut.

Badam Katli

almond fudge diamonds

INGREDIENTS

2 cups almonds

¾ cup sugar

½ tsp cardamom powder

A few strands of saffron

1 tbsp ghee

2-3 thin silver foil sheets

METHOD

Soak almonds in hot water for 10 minutes. Drain, peel, and pat dry. Grind to a fine powder. Place sugar in a thick-bottomed pan and add enough water to cover the surface. Cook on high heat to make a syrup of 2-3 string consistency. Mix cardamom powder and saffron in a little water and add to syrup. Add ground almonds and continue stirring. When sugar and almonds are well mixed, remove from heat (approx. 2-3 minutes).

Grease the counter or work surface with ghee. Turn out the almond mixture on to the surface and immediately start rolling it out with a greased rolling pin to the required thickness. Even out the mixture and press silver foil to cover the top. Cut diagonally to make diamond shapes. Leave to cool to room temperature. Remove with a sharp, flat spoon. Store in an airtight container.

Makes 24 pieces

Sitafal ni Basundi

custard apple dessert

INGREDIENTS

- 1½ litres (6 cups) full fat milk
- 6 tbsp sugar
- 1 cup custard apple pulp
- A pinch of cardamom powder

To garnish

- Toasted and sliced pistachios

METHOD

In a thick-bottomed pan, heat the milk with sugar on low heat, stirring occasionally until sugar has melted. Increase heat to medium and cook until it reduces to half. During this process, do not stir, but scrape off the milk fat which gathers on the sides. Remove from heat and cool completely.

Add the custard apple pulp, cardamom powder and mix well. Chill for 2 hours. Garnish with pistachios and serve.

Serves 4-6

Note: You can replace custard apples with any other fruit such as peaches, mangoes, oranges, kiwis etc.

Doodh Pak

rice pudding

INGREDIENTS

- 1 litre milk
- 1 tbsp raw rice, washed
- 1 tsp ghee
- 125 gm rock sugar, crushed
- ½ tsp saffron threads
- ½ tsp cardamom powder
- ½ tsp grated nutmeg
- ¼ cup almonds, blanched and sliced

METHOD

Boil milk in a thick-bottomed pan. Rub rice with ghee and add to milk. Cook on low heat till it begins to thicken.

Add sugar, and bring to a boil and cook again till the milk reduces in quantity by a third. Add saffron, cardamom and nutmeg. Remove from heat and add almonds.

Serve hot.

Serves 4

Sherdi na Gola

sugarcane sorbet

INGREDIENTS

1 litre sugarcane juice
1 tsp ginger juice
1 tsp lemon juice
1 cup vanilla ice cream
1 medium melon

METHOD

Blend all the three juices and vanilla ice cream in a blender. Pour into an ice cream container and freeze for 2-3 hours. Remove from freezer and blend again. Freeze the blended mixture again for 3-4 hours or overnight.

Cut the melon in half and scoop out the flesh. Use the flesh in another recipe. Chill the melon shell. Scoop the sorbet and fill it into halved melon and serve.

Serves 4-6

Kesar Peda

saffron-flavoured milk fudge

INGREDIENTS

- 400 gm *mawa/khoya*, grated
- 100 gm cottage cheese, grated
- 100 gm cashew nuts, ground to a powder
- 2½ cups (approx.) powdered sugar
- ½ tsp cardamom powder
- ½ tsp saffron threads
- 2-3 tbsp crushed pistachios

METHOD

Lightly mix together in a bowl, the *mawa*, cottage cheese and powdered cashew nuts. Add the sugar, a little at a time. Mix gently, making sure that the natural oils do not ooze out of the mixture. Add cardamom and saffron. Shape tablespoons of the mixture on your palm into small balls, and press lightly press to make a dent in the center. Press a few chopped pistachios in the middle. Store in a cool place.

Makes 50 *pedas*

Mug Dal Seera

split green gram sweet

INGREDIENTS

- 1 cup skinless split green gram
- A few saffron strands
- 1 cup warmed milk
- 6 tbsp ghee
- 1 cup warm water
- 1¼ cups sugar
- ½ tsp cardamom powder

To garnish

- Almond and pistachio slivers

METHOD

Soak the split gram in water for 3-4 hours. Drain and grind to a coarse paste using very little water. Dissolve the saffron in 1 tablespoon of warm milk and set aside.

Melt the ghee in a wide non-stick pan. Add the *dal* paste and stir the mixture continuously on a low heat till it becomes golden brown. Add the warm milk and warm water and cook, stirring continuously till absorbed. Add the sugar and cook on a low heat till the ghee separates. Add the saffron and cardamom powder and mix well. Serve hot, garnished with slivers of almonds and pistachios.

Serves 8-10

Lychee Kulfi

INGREDIENTS

1½ litres milk

⅓ cup sugar

½ tin (200 gm) sweetened condensed milk

1 cup lychee pulp, strained (approx. 16-18 pieces)

METHOD

Heat the milk in a heavy-bottomed pan until it reduces to three-fourth its original quantity. Add sugar and boil again till it is reduced to half its original quantity. Remove from heat and set aside to cool.

Add condensed milk and lychee pulp. Mix well. Fill *kulfi* moulds with this mixture and freeze overnight. To remove *kulfi* from the moulds, rub the mould with both your palms and slightly loosen the *kulfi*. Serve in a small ice cream cone or a bowl.

Variation: Replace lychees with fruit pulp of your choice such as custard apple, mango, mixed dried fruit, strawberry etc.

To use ready *kulfi* mix, reduce milk to ½ litre, omit sugar and reduce condensed milk to ¼ cup. Make as directed on the box, cool and then add the fruit pulp.

Makes 6-8 *kulfis*

Lychee Kulfi (recipe on adjacent page)

Gol Papdi (recipe on page 178)

Shrikhand (recipe on adjacent page)

Shrikhand

saffron-flavoured yogurt

INGREDIENTS

250 gm plain yogurt
3-4 tbsp sugar OR
1½ tsp sugar substitute
A few saffron threads
½ tsp cardamom powder

To garnish

Thinly sliced almonds and pistachios

METHOD

Tie the yogurt up in a muslin cloth and hang over a bowl for 1 hour, or till all the water has drained out. Place the drained yogurt in a bowl and mix in the sugar. Pass through a strainer to get a smooth consistency.

Mix saffron threads in a little water and add to the yogurt along with cardamom powder. Mix well and transfer to a serving bowl. Sprinkle the nuts and chill in the refrigerator until ready to serve.

Serves 2

Gol Papdi

wholewheat flour and jaggery fudge

INGREDIENTS

½ cup ghee
1 cup coarse wholewheat flour
½-¾ cup finely chopped jaggery
2-3 tbsp milk
¼ tsp cardamom powder

To garnish

Sliced almonds and pistachios and poppy seeds

METHOD

Heat ghee in a *kadai*, and roast flour on low heat until dark brown. Remove from heat and add chopped jaggery, milk and cardamom powder. Mix well. Return to stove and cook until jaggery has melted completely. Remove from heat and transfer to greased 7-inch stainless steel plate.

Smooth the surface with the back of a greased flat spoon. Sprinkle with almonds, pistachios and poppy seeds. Leave to cool completely. Cut into 1-inch squares and serve.

Makes 16-18 *papdis*

Khopra Pak

coconut fudge

INGREDIENTS

5 cups freshly grated coconut

½ cup fresh cream, skimmed from top of milk

1 tbsp ghee

1½ cups sugar

1 cup condensed milk

½ tsp saffron powder

1 tsp cardamom powder

2 tbsp pistachios, chopped

METHOD

In a large bowl, mix together coconut and cream and set aside for half an hour. Grease a 14-inch stainless steel plate with a high rim (*thali*), with ghee. Heat a large *kadai*; add coconut-cream mixture and dry-roast it for 8-10 minutes. When the coconut looks a little dry, add sugar and condensed milk and mix well. Cook on a medium heat for 15-20 minutes. Check the consistency with your fingers: if it forms a thick syrup of one-string consistency, then take the pan off the heat.

Add saffron powder mixed with a little milk and cardamom powder. Mix well, and pour into the greased plate. Smooth the surface with the back of a greased spoon. Sprinkle pistachios on top. Leave to cool completely. Cut into 1-inch squares or diamonds. Take the pieces out of the plate with the help of a flat spoon and transfer to a serving plate. Decorate with rose petals.

Make approx. 34 pieces

Jalebi

sweet syrupy spirals

INGREDIENTS

- 2 cups plain flour
- 1½ cups plain yogurt
- ½ cup warm water
- 3 tbsp hot ghee
- ½ kg sugar
- 1 tsp cardamom powder
- 1 tsp saffron powder
- Ghee for deep-frying

To garnish

- 3-4 tbsp almonds and pistachios, sliced
- A few rose petals

METHOD

Mix together the flour, yogurt, warm water and hot ghee. Beat the mixture vigorously till smooth. Cover and set aside in a warm place. If the weather is cold you will need to prepare this 2 nights in advance. Cook sugar with just enough water to make a syrup of one-string consistency. Add cardamom and saffron powders and place on low heat to keep it warm.

When ready to serve, heat the ghee in a *kadai*. Beat the *jalebi* mixture till it is of a dropping consistency. Fill a cylindrical bottle with a small nozzle with this mixture. Squeeze out spiral shapes small distance apart into the hot ghee. Make 4-5 *jalebis* at a time. Turn them over occasionally with the help of tongs. When they are golden, remove and place them in the hot syrup 5-7 minutes. Transfer to a serving plate. Garnish with almonds, pistachios and rose petals and serve at once.

Serves 6-8

Keri ni barfi, Pista na Cup ma

mango barfi in pistachio cups

INGREDIENTS

For barfi

250 gm Alphonso mango pulp

250 gm sugar

1 tbsp ghee

250 gm *mawa/khoya*

For pistachio cups

250 gm shelled pistachios

200 gm sugar

100 ml water

A pinch of cardamom powder

1 tbsp ghee

1 tbsp arrowroot flour

To garnish

Slivered almonds

METHOD

For barfi

Mix mango pulp and sugar together in a heavy-bottomed pan. Stir until sugar melts. Cook on low heat for 5-10 minutes. Remove from heat and set aside. In a small frying pan, heat ghee and fry *khoya* on a low heat till slightly golden. Add to the mango mixture. Return the pan to the heat and cook gently, stirring continuously, until thick. Remove from heat and set aside.

For pistachio cups

Place pistachios in hot water for 5-10 minutes and peel. Pat dry and powder them in a grinder. Heat sugar and water in a pan until dissolved. Remove from heat and add cardamom powder and powdered pistachios. Mix well. Heat ghee in a small frying pan and add pistachio mixture and arrowroot and cook on low heat until thick. Remove and refrigerate this mixture until completely cold. Divide the pistachio mixture into 30 portions and shape into balls first and then into small bowls. Arrange on a serving tray and place 1 tablespoon of mango *barfi* mixture in each one. Garnish with almonds and chill until ready to serve.

Makes 30 cups

Mohanthaal

roasted gram flour fudge

INGREDIENTS

2 cups coarse gram flour

1 cup ghee

1 cup grated *mawa/khoya*

1 tsp cardamom powder

For sugar syrup

1½ cups sugar

1 cup water

2 tbsp milk

To garnish

4 tbsp chopped almonds and pistachios

METHOD

Place the gram flour in a bowl. Heat the ghee and pour half of it over the gram flour. Rub the ghee into the gram flour till the mixture resembles breadcrumbs. Add to the remaining hot ghee in a *kadai* and cook till mixture is golden brown, stirring continuously. Add the grated *mawa* and cardamom powder and stir for about 5 to 7 minutes. Remove from the heat and allow to cool till it becomes lukewarm.

For sugar syrup

Mix the sugar with water in pan and simmer for 10 minutes. To the milk, add 2 tablespoons water and pour this into the boiling sugar syrup. This is done to clarify the syrup of impurities. Gently remove the grey layer which forms on top with a slotted spoon. Cook on low heat till the syrup attains a one-thread consistency. Keep the syrup hot.

To make mohanthaal

Pour the hot sugar syrup over the cooked gram flour mixture and stir well. Pour into a greased 9-inch *thali* (plate with a 1-inch high rim). Sprinkle chopped almonds and pistachios and leave to set for 4 to 5 hours. Cut into 1-inch squares. Serve at room temperature.

Makes 1 kg

Keri ane Custard nu Pudding

mango parfait

INGREDIENTS

- 2 cups milk
- ½ cup sugar
- 2 tbsp cornflour
- 1½ tbsp unflavoured gelatine, mixed with ¼ cup water
- ½ tsp lemon juice
- ¾ cup fresh cream, beaten
- ½ cup mango pulp
- 2 medium Alphonso mangoes, peeled and chopped

To garnish

- A few chopped mango pieces

METHOD

In a medium pan, mix together milk, sugar and cornflour and bring to a boil, stirring continuously. Reduce heat and simmer until thick. Remove from heat and set aside to cool. In a small pan, heat the gelatine mixture until dissolved. Add lemon juice and set aside to cool. Beat the lemon mixture into the cooled milk along with the cream. Divide the mixture into two parts. Add mango pulp to one part and half the chopped mangoes to the other.

In individual stemmed glasses, layer both the custards alternately with remaining fresh mango pieces in between, forming 3 layers. Garnish with chopped mango. Chill in the refrigerator for 1-2 hours before serving.

Serves 6

Annanas ni Barfi

pineapple fudge

INGREDIENTS

1 cup *khoya/mawa*

1 cup cottage cheese

½ cup powdered sugar

A few strands of saffron, mixed with milk

⅓ cup finely chopped pineapple

To garnish

Silver foil

METHOD

Grate *khoya* and heat in a small frying pan until it separates a little. Cool. Similarly grate and cook cottage cheese in a pan until dry. Cool. Mix together *khoya* and cottage cheese with sugar. Rub well to make soft mixture. Add saffron and mix well.

Spread half the mixture in a tray in rectangular shape. Sprinkle pineapple pieces over and cover with the remaining half of *khoya*-cottage cheese mixture. Press gently to make a neat surface. Cut into diamond shapes and arrange each piece on a paper cup. Serve either at room temperature or cold. Alternatively, you can make small balls of the *khoya*-cottage cheese mixture and press to form a disc. Stuff a few pieces of pineapple in each one and give it either a round or oblong shape. Place them on paper cups and garnish with silver foil.

Makes 10-12 *barfis*

Glossary

ENGLISH	HINDI	GUJARATI
Amaranth	Chouli/chavli	Chouli
Amaranth grain	Rajgira/ramdana	Rajgara
Aniseed	Saunf	Variyali
Arrowroot	Paniphal, tikora	Shingoda
Asafoetida	Hing	Hing
Basil	Tulsi	Tulsi
Beaten rice	Poha	Pawa
Bengal gram	Chana	Channa
Bengal gram, roasted	Bhuna chana	Daalia
Bengal gram, split	Chane ki dal	Channa ni dal
Black gram, skinless, split	Dhuli udad dal	Udad ni dal
Black gram, whole	Sabut udad	Kala udad
Black peppercorns	Kali mirch	Miri
Black salt	Kala namak	Sanchal
Black-eyed beans	Lobia	Chawli
Bottle gourd	Lauki/ghia/doodhi	Dudhi
Brinjal	Baingan	Ringan
Broad beans	Sem	Papdi
Broad beans, shelled, tender	Sem ke dane	Papdi dana
Brown chickpeas	Lal chana	Laal channa
Buckwheat flour	Kuttu atta	Kuti no lot
Buttermilk	Chaas	Chaas
Capsicum	Shimla mirch	Shimla mirch
Caraway seeds	Shah jeera	Shah jeera
Cardamoms	Elaichi	Elchi
Carom seeds	Ajwain	Ajmo
Chickpeas	Kabuli chana	Kabuli channa
Chillies, round, red	Boria mirch	Boriya marcha
Cinnamon	Dalchini	Tuj
Clarified butter	Ghee	Ghee
Coconut	Nariyal	Khopru
Coriander seeds	Dhania	Kothmir na dana
Corn kernels	Makai ke dane	Makai na dana
Cottage cheese	Paneer	Paneer

ENGLISH	HINDI	GUJARATI
Cracked buckwheat	Kuttu	Kuttu-dara
Cracked millet	Bajra ka dalia	Bajri dalia
Cracked wheat	Dalia	Ganu na fada
Cumin seeds	Jeera	Jeeru
Curry leaves	Kadhi patte	Limda
Custard apple	Sitafal	Sitafal
Dill leaves	Suva bhaji	Suva bhaji
Dried mango powder	Amchur	Amchur
Drumsticks	Saijan ki phalli	Sargva ni singh
Elephant's foot yam	Zimikand	Suran
Fenugreek leaves	Methi	Methi
Fenugreek leaves, dried	Kasoori methi	Kasoori methi
Fenugreek seeds	Methi dana	Methi dana
Field beans	Sem	Val
Finger Millet	Ragi	Ragi
Garlic	Lasan	Lasan
Ginger	Adrak	Adu
Gram flour	Besan	Channa no lot
Green chillies	Hari mirch	Lila mirchi
Green gram, fresh	Hara chana	Lila channa
Green gram, skinless split	Dhuli mung dal	Mug ni dal
Green gram, split	Chilkewali mung dal	Lili mug ni dal
Green gram, whole	Sabut moong	Mug
Green millet, fresh		Ponk
Green peas	Matar	Vatana
Indian sorrel/roselle leaves	Khatta bhaji	Khatti bhaji
Ivy gourd	Kundru	Tindora
Jaggery	Gud	Gol
Ladies' fingers/Okra	Bhindi	Bhinda
Lemon grass	Chai ki patti	Lili chai
Lentils, split	Masoor ki dal	Masoor ni dal
Maize flour	Makkai ka atta	Makai no lot
Mango ginger	Aam haldi	Amba haldi
Millet	Bajra	Bajri
Moth beans	Moth	Muth
Mustard	Rai	Rai

ENGLISH	HINDI	GUJARATI
Mustard grains, split	Rai ki dal	Rai ni dal
Nigella seeds (onion seeds)	Kalonji	Kalonji
Nutmeg	Jaiphal	Jaiphal
Onion	Pyaaz	Kanda
Peanuts	Moongphali	Shing
Pigeon peas, fresh	Hara toovar/hara arhar	Tuver lilva
Pigeon peas, split	Toovar dal/arhar dal	Tuvar dal
Pine nuts	Chilgoza	Neja
Purple yam	Ratalu	Kand
Pistachio	Pista	Pista
Plain flour	Maida	Maida
Pointed gourd	Parval	Parval
Pomegranate	Anaar	Dadam
Poppy seeds	Khuskhus	Khuskhus
Potatoes	Aloo	Batata
Potassium carbonate/pearl ash	Javakhar	Papadkhar/kharo
Puffed lotus seeds	Makhana	Makhana
Raisins	Kishmish	Kismis
Ridge gourd	Turai	Turia
Rock salt	Sendha namak	Sindhalu mithu
Rock sugar	Mishri	Khadi saakar
Saffron	Kesar	Kesar
Sago	Sabudana	Sabudana
Semolina	Rawa/sooji	Ravo
Sesame seeds	Til	Tul
Snake gourd	Chachinda	Pandola
Sorghum flour	Jowar atta	Jawar no lot
Spring onions (scallions)	Hara pyaaz	Lila kanda
Sugarcane	Ganna	Sherdi
Sunflower seeds	Surya mukhi ke beej	Surya mukhi
Water chestnut	Singhara	Singoda
White peas, dried	Safed matar	Vatana
White radish	Safed mooli	Mula
Wholewheat flour	Atta	Ghun no lot
Yogurt	Dahi	Dahi

Glossary of Terms

Appetiser	A first course of a meal of tidbits, drinks or cocktails
Bake	To cook in an oven by dry heat
Blanch	To immerse briefly in boiling water
Broil	To cook directly over or above heat e.g. to grill
Croquettes	A soft mixture of vegetables and seasoning, rolled into oval shapes coated with bread crumbs or vermicelli and fried
Deep-fry	To fry in plenty of fat
Drain	To remove excess liquid or fat from food, usually with the help of a colander or by placing on absorbent paper
Drizzle	To pour liquid slowly in a thin stream over food, e.g. vegetables with olive oil
Dry-roast	To heat/lightly fry without fat; usually spices, on a griddle (*tawa*)
Dust	To sprinkle lightly with flour or sugar
Fritter	A portion of batter-coated food, deep-fried until crisp
Garnish	To decorate a dish
Gelatine	Unflavoured gelatine granules used to set a mixture
Grease	To coat the surface of a dish with fat to prevent sticking
Grill	To cook over or under dry heat; barbecue
Marinate	To soak an ingredient before cooking in a mixture of spices or souring agents such as lemon juice or yogurt
Parboil	To partially cook by boiling briefly in water
Purée	To make a smooth pulp of vegetables or fruit usually in a blender
Sauté	To fry quickly in a little hot oil
Seasoning	Salt, pepper, spices, herbs etc added to give depth of flavour
Sieve	To rub or press moist or dry food through a sieve
Simmer	To cook food gently in liquid just below boiling point
Steam	To cook an ingredient in the steam of boiling water without it touching water
Stir-fry	To fry quickly over high heat in a lightly oiled pan (as in a wok), while stirring continuously
Temper	To heat spices in oil before adding to a dish
Toss	To mix ingredients in a quick, light way, till thoroughly blended
Vinegar	Generally made from malt, cider, sugarcane or grape juice to add sour taste to many dishes
Whisk	To whip or beat ingredients to incorporate air and make it light e.g. egg whites, yogurt or cream